THE CREATIVE

2

THE CREATIVE

2

Communicating with Brush and Pen
in Graphic Design

Richard Emery

ROCKPORT PUBLISHERS • ROCKPORT, MASSACHUSETTS
Distributed by North Light Books, Cincinnati, Ohio

First published in the United States of America by:
Rockport Publishers, Inc.
146 Granite Street
Rockport, Massachusetts 01966
Telephone: (508) 546-9590
Fax: (508) 546-7141
Telex: 5106019284 ROCKORT PUB

First Published in Germany by Rockport Publishers, Inc. for:
Nippan
Nippon Shuppan Hanbai Deutschland GmbH
Krefelder Str. 85
D-40549 Dusseldorf
Telephone: (0211) 504 8089
Fax: (0211) 504 9326

Distributed to the book trade and art trade in the U.S. and Canada by:
North Light, an imprint of
F & W Publications
1507 Dana Avenue
Cincinnati, Ohio 45207
Telephone: (513) 531-2222

Other Distribution by:
Rockport Publishers, Inc.
Rockport, Massachusetts 01966

ISBN 1-56496-078-1

10 9 8 7 6 5 4 3 2 1

Designer: Richard Emery
Production Manager: Barbara States
Production Assistant: Pat O'Maley

Printed in Singapore

Contents

Foreword   7

Freehand:
Viablility in the Graphics Business   8

The Art Speaks For Itself   19

Paul Shaw	20
Colleen	26
Sherry Bringham	32
John Sayles	38
Edward Vartanian	44
Julian Waters	48
Jane Dill	54
Terry Louie	60
Mike Quon	64
Daniel Riley	68
Jean Evans	74
Claude Dieterich A.	78
Larry Brady	82
Ivan Angelic	88
John Stevens	94
Richard Lipton	100
James Fedor	104
Georgia Deaver	110
Frank Riccio	114
Susan Skarsgard	118
Joey Hannaford	122
Anthony Bloch	126
Nancy Culmone	132
Raphael Boguslav	138
Bonnie Spiegel	142
Sheila Waters	146
Brenda Walton	150
Iskra Johnson	154
Miscellany	159

Gallery   179

Index   190

Foreword

I n the first volume of *The Creative Stroke,* the primary effort was to demonstrate just how inclusive the application of freehand graphics is in the communications industry. It can often intuitively touch the creative center of a problem more directly than any other method. It has a real connection to the inner reactive nature of the viewer. All this is shown again here in volume two.

One of the most interesting results of the first go-around was that each of the artists has such a wide range of expression. They show such diversity of style from situation to situation, and seem less interested in promoting a specific style than discovering appropriate and meaningful communication. Thus emerged a natural format for the content of a new volume, *The Creative Stroke 2.*

Two considerations immediately come to mind. First, many of the artists integrate their work through a wide range of media and must therefore make accommodations to the demands of production materials and specifications. The need to keep artwork within differing restrictions guarantees variety, and, since the hand is almost limitless in its possibilities, this need certainly does not seem to be a constraint.

Secondly, they are exposed to products and situations that are very different from each other both in imagery and in content. Though products and services can be placed in generalized categories, they still possess their separate identities and must be understood in that light.

As *The Creative Stroke 2* began to take shape, it became apparent that there was a need to invite the contributors to talk about not only the diversity of their expression but also the very process they use to produce their work. If, in fact, the results of their efforts have an intuitive nature, then it must also be true that the process of creating them follows along the same subjective path. Since each artist has a disctinctive approach to creativity, a questionnaire was drawn up and presented to them. It discussed the basic format for an article concerning the design process from beginning to end.

The results from this invitation were both remarkable and illuminating. No two artists revealed exactly the same philosophy or approach to the creative process, and yet what they reported seemed to genuinely support the editorial scheme of the article. Many of them decried the efforts of those in the communications industry who attempt to reign in or dictate the end results of their efforts. They talked of sometimes feeling constrained to the point of losing the personal touch that their talent offers. Yet these experiences did not diminish their commitment to the real challenge of their art.

Sometimes the constraints on creativity come from shared production, where an artist has only a piece of the puzzle and has little or no influence on the remaining parts. Though a certain sterility can creep into the art, many of the respondents stated that shared creativity was not necessarily a problem. If they were included in the overall problem-solving strategy, their work could be successfully integrated and their talents fully utilized.

As you proceed on through this book you will be amazed and delighted at the successful integration of the freehand artists' work into the overall design strategies. They have been selected for just this reason, and their work truly affirms the premise of this volume: flexibility, adaptability, and the viable nature of freehand expression.

We hope that you will be inspired to a greater appreciation of the world of graphic design, or to a new and expanded approach to your own artistry. Much has been said and much has been written, but nothing can compare with seeing the results.

Richard S. Emery
President and Creative Director
Richard Emery Design, Inc.

Viability in the Graphics Business

The following article was compiled from conversations with and questions presented to some of today's best known freehand artists and calligraphers. Much gratitude goes out to them for their contributions.

Who knows? The basic impulse to write/draw comes from places inside us that no one can really explain." This was the response of John Stevens to the question of motivation in his work. His statement reaches to the core of what is unique about immersing oneself in the art of freehand expression, and why it is so important to the communications industry. Subjectivity, intuitive responses, felt rather than rationalized impulses: these all seem to be common grounds for meaningful freehand expression and therefore provide an answer to where artists get their creative ideas.

But this is just the beginning. If we are to understand the significance of freehand graphics as a communications tool, we must examine the whole process. The full reach of successful graphic communications extends well beyond the first subjective touch. There is more to an idea than just impulse. "The 'product' is a visual one," says Nancy Culmone. "So many decisions can only be made visually." This then presupposes a need for a flexible yet working structure to realize the completion of an idea. The following generalized structural conditions are suggested for approaching freehand graphics:

1. Motivation

2. Exploration

3. Comprehension

4. Experimentation

5. Actualization

Motivation refers to what excites and motivates the designer to use the freehand approach to solve graphic design problems. *Exploration* is the activity used to discover the true nature of a problem and to search for its definition. *Comprehension* means fully understanding the results of this exploration and developing a workable articulation to apply to the continuing process. *Experimentation* refers to the actual hands-on application of this knowledge through various approaches to freehand expression. *Actualization* is the time needed for final decision-making, isolation of the appropriate application, and the finished rendering of the results.

Many artists and designers will find that they fit comfortably within these conditions. Others would wish to change the sequence or combine two or more of them. Nevertheless, this set of conditions provides a springboard for understanding just how they work and how they produce their wonderfully creative and original ideas.

Again responding to **Motivation**, John Stevens says, "Apparently drawing/mark-making is a language we artists feel compelled to become fluid in. Without such expression, something feels 'wrong'. It is as if we are moving toward becoming fluent in a yet undiscovered but ancient language inside us which requires constant practice, awareness, etc." It is as though we are discussing an innate part of the artist and not a part of some conscious reality. This is perhaps what ultimately separates out the freehand

artist and defines the difference from other design approaches.

"There is a nuance of voice," says Jean Evans, "that's not available otherwise." Her use of the word "voice" seems to validate what this discussion presumes, that whatever processes the different freehand artists follow to complete their work, it all begins somewhere in a common search for "voice," some personal intuitive expression that will communicate throughout the development of the art.

"Freehand graphics brings a living and animated character to language capable of expressing the concept or value through the immediate interpretation of the artist." Thus Anthony Bloch describes his feelings about graphics and language. Communication must come first from some immediate subjective response before the translation to

This design was created for an Argentine graphic design magazine, tipoGráfica, *by Claude Dieterich A. Through design he has given these bits of calligraphy a great sense of freedom.*

graphics takes place. The very nature of this response is well defined when the artist Colleen says, ". . .the sentiment I hear most frequently at the juncture of the artist/client relationship is 'I'm looking for a human touch.' What better, more unique solution; uniqueness wedded to strength and beauty will certainly capture and hold a greater audience." Certainly the "human touch" is what arrives at the very beginning and is what motivates the artist's creativity. Terry Louie adds, "The human heart responds instantly to human touch."

Basic human responses are triggered by this touch. An example is response to *movement*. Joey Hannaford says, "It

Iskra Johnson produced the freehand title for this poster for UNEP. It has a direct relationship with the illustration by Braldt Bralds

is one of our most intrinsic characteristics as humans, whose sight is our sense of primary importance, to be attracted to anything that moves. As a college student I often attended parties where a television was left on, the sound turned all the way down, music on the stereo blasting. My friends and I would sit in a room, having entire conversations unrelated to anything happening on the television screen, but still with all eyes glued to the motion on the screen. We couldn't help but follow the motion with our eyes. I feel that handcrafted elements within graphic design serve the same purpose. The movement implied by a fluid or rough line, obviously handcrafted, creates a visceral communication, many times subliminal in its impact, but always drawing the eye to follow its movement. . . .I usually turn to hand lettering as a way of introducing movement and energy into a design that has become slightly static due to a very conservative use of type within a grid."

Though this reaches into the next suggested step in the process, it seems that the human response mechanism is also touched subjectively by the experience of contemporary living. In discussing the artist/client relationship, Paul Shaw states, "These clients often need only a single word, a phrase or set of headlines. These words are inevitably described in either vague or ambiguous terms: they must be fresh, contemporary, youthful, unique, new, spontaneous, etc." This is where the intuitive hand can come to full flower, creating real but subjective communication with a few appropriate strokes of the brush or pen.

Another motivational pull seems to be the need for growth and change. Marsha Brady, in discussing her calligraphic work, says, "Many times the freehand, expressive solution may stem from attempting to break from the cliché, or just playing with the tools." One's personal artistic growth may well be a major motivation and a catalyst for direction and artistic identity. Very much related to this idea is a comment made by Susan Skarsgard. "In my own personal work (not commercial) my motivation is usually quite different. I may choose to undertake a project based on the inspiration of a meaningful text, or a technique that I would like to explore, or using materials and tools that I have never tried

This design produced for the Type Directors Club displays the wonderful freehand talent of Mike Quon. The strokes create the negative space allowing the letter form to appear.

before, or a reproduction method that is unfamiliar to me. . . .That is why I value and always strive to devote time each year to making art that is for me and my own goals alone. I believe it enhances and effects the quality of my commercial work as well. I see it as creative research."

It follows that once motivated the artist will then seek out the true nature of the problem to be solved. This could be called the area of **Exploration,** a time to search for some meaningful definition of content. "To me," says John Stevens, "exploration is working with a problem until it gets lodged into our subconscious where real inspiration takes place. Then a unique point of view transcending simple logic or linear approach is possible." When working commercially it involves client discussion and questioning.

Daniel Riley, of Riley Design Associates, shows how a simple use of the freehand stroke successfully frames a piece of art and adds focus to this delightful T-shirt design.

"In trying to elicit more information to clear up any vagueness and ambiguity," John continues, "this process sometimes yields 'the answer' within minutes or, at other times, it takes many hours."

Exploration can mean different things to different people. To reach the same kinds of objectives, artists may employ thinking and questioning, as Jean Evans says, "with in-depth conversation to get to the heart of the project," or, as Larry Brady suggests, "Intellectualizing visual problems can often lead to predictable results. One does what one knows, or what is expected. It is the exploration of ideas with materials in hand, being shaped by hand that can lead to exciting discoveries and thereby to better ways of defining the problem, which usually provides the most interesting and original solution." It is obvious that any approach to exploration that inspires and stimulates the artist is valid and in fact demonstrates the special nature of the very process we are discussing. Nancy Culmone says,

"Exploration revolves around the 'purpose' and uses of the final product. Is it a logo or a letterhead? Intimate or public — *why* is this needed." She is addressing the concern of all artists and designers at this stage of the process, and it must certainly be a part of discovering the true nature of the problem to be solved.

Also, there is the commitment of the artist to the task. "By constantly thinking of a design problem," says Terry Louie, "even while riding a bus or sifting through related material, an idea emerges." Colleen says, "Sometimes I forget that simply sitting and closing my eyes — awake, dreaming — can assist greatly in this compilation and sifting stage. I do find this not-hands-on time is when it's O.K. to stop, think about the job at hand and let possible solutions arise." Joey Hannaford makes an interesting observation on the commitment and integrity of her designing when she says, "The active energy of hand lettering is not always appropriate. I have to evaluate this seriously within my own thought processes, as I want to be sure that I am not turning to a hand lettering solution merely as a crutch or as something that I prefer to do for my own enjoyment, rather than for the integrity of the piece." This does not downplay the importance of freehand expression, but merely demonstrates the commitment to honest appraisal and concern for the integrity of the final solution.

Sherry Bringham remarks, "With exploration comes discovery and definition, not only for the designer but also for the calligrapher. We often think we've taken something as far as it can go until we are pushed into a new catharsis, and then we find that this process is the source for new ideas."

"Comprehension is a never-ending learning experience," says Jane Dill. Sherry Bringham adds, "The big picture (comprehension) presumes that the designer understands the process." What they seem to be saying is that this is a critical spot in the evolution of an idea. When the artist presumes to have a real grasp on the content, then she or he is accepting the risk to begin implementation. Concerning the risk factor, Colleen says, "I have a favorite quote on my drawing board. The words are Jay Maisel's (photographer) and must trust that something will come: 'Work hard, be a perfectionist and always be prepared to fail before you succeed.' The first two are easy for me. It's the last I need to be reminded of on an hourly basis."

This stage is not so much an involvement of time as it is representative of the moment an artist feels secure with the subjective content of the project. When comprehension is secure, articulation through trial and experimentation begins.

Experimentation is when the real fun and work begin. This means trying different expressions along with further variations on them. Joey Hannaford addresses this when she says, "At this state I will create a very rough version of the hand lettering, or hand-produced design element, scan it in, play

In this spot for Hoffmann & Angelic Design, Ivan Angelic successfully produces the feel of "lively characters" with his bouncing script.

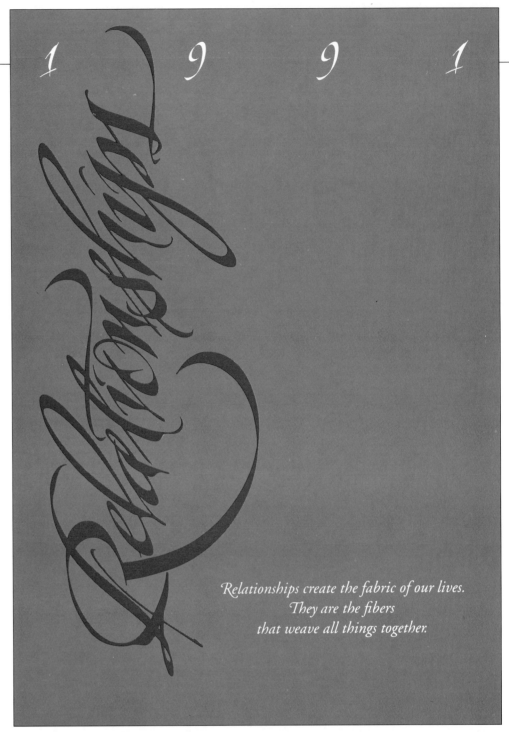

with position and scale and have a more specific idea of where I want the hand lettering to 'go'." Larry Brady also acknowledges this by saying, "The chance of arriving at a good solution to a problem is enhanced by the 'hands-on' exploration of many ideas and the process of evaluation as work progresses. Cross-fertilization reduces the chance of soporific designs and worn-out decisions."

"Experimentation to me," says John Stevens, "refers to the ongoing dialog we should keep of our work without thought to tangible results. It feeds the imagination as well as feeding on the imagination. Basically, it keeps your work from being derivative or *dry*. Experimentation is wet! Juicy!"

Since this was the area that received the most liberal response, the following is a list of some responses without comment. They provide an interesting comparison of differing ideas and styles while underscoring the common experience – having fun:

"The fun part! Using different tools and styles and papers (brush marker on paper towel for 'Melónge') and just playing at the rough stage – sometimes that energy can be captured at this stage and with very few refinements can become final art (see Julian's 'Relationships')."
    – Jane Dill

"The externalization of concepts through the means of hand processes provides a vital element in the creative process. It puts distance between object and creator and allows for a more detached, unbiased view of the work in progress. Without the external form of our ideas to respond to, the feedback loop is severed and interrelationships cannot be discovered. Most importantly, the wonderful accidents that happen in this type of activity, which often result in exciting new solutions to design problems, would never happen."
    – Larry Brady

Relationships create the fabric of our lives.
They are the fibers
that weave all things together.

"Experimentation leads to developing the overall idea. If the project is done for a client, usually a series of layouts are prepared for presentation. The calligraphy may be the key element or a small part of the project. It may be a wildly expressive piece for an art poster or an exact, totally legible part of a packaging design. Art projects allow the calligrapher certain freedoms, and often the piece works itself around the lettering; packaging projects and their size definitions bring their own rules. For instance, rough calligraphy is often put into several designs which go into

(top)
Julian Waters created the lettering design for this highly expressive cover for a calendar for S&S Graphics, Inc. The art director was Tony Fitch.

(bottom)
This rough spongy style was created by Jane Dill for a raspberry watermellon wine spritzer for Boku. (Design Firm: Source Inc., Art Director: Michael Livolf)

Alice B. Theatre presents

Camille

by **Charles Ludlam**

October 9 - November 7, 1993
Pay-What-You-Will Performance October 20

at the **Ethnic Cultural Theatre**
3940 Brooklyn Ave. N.E.
For tickets call **322-5423**

Poster by Modern Dog
Printing by Two Dimensions

Below is an excellent example of a "tortured" script to accompany the art on this theatre poster for the Alice B. Theatre. Michael Strassburger designed and illustrated this piece for the design firm Modern Dog.

the computer, and letters may be pushed, pulled, extended, compressed, etc., to fit a certain space. The layout often returns barely recognizable, but the space and design are determined, and the calligrapher now works to perfect the rough computer image of his own work."
— Sherry Bringham

"If I've done my homework, I've generally got a nice set of self-articulated 'specs' for a job. They're like a sturdy, mental safety net, or a pair of crutches on which I can lean as I step up to this new task. Like most people, beginnings can stymie me; this safety net of givens (scale, style, use, attitude, color, etc.) can keep my visual space wide open allowing for tremendous freedom. Tools, too, play an integral part in fostering spontaneity, and right now – in the experimentation stage – I do not want my brain hampering the process.

"Now to begin. This is the exciting, lonely, and gratifying time. Once the process of working up concept roughs has begun, time must stop it. If I can stay at the board through the typical, stiff, initial sketches (yawn, don't I need to go downstairs for something – anything?! I'm completely exhausted and I've just had a night's sleep), if I can stay the anxiety and keep working, pretty soon the solutions are each demanding their own sheet of paper, one rising up before the last is quite done. A number of years ago Raphael Boguslav talked about beginning a project with an entire ream of large good quality paper at his side. That image was a wonderfully permissive one I continue to hold dear, as much energy goes into keeping the stern, nay-saying parents at bay during this stage."
— Colleen

"The product is a visual one – so many decisions can only be made visually, through visual thought – doing and looking depending on stage 3. This can be very subtle variations and experiments, or a great variety of extremes can be explored in the search for the right visual expression (how does one express peace or wetness or wild?). There are an infinite variety of solutions – sometimes it is just time to stop and choose."
— Nancy Culmone

"When the client looks at my samples, I like to get more than a simple yes or no. I like to know if any individual characters are problematical, how the lettering will fit the designer's layout, if they want the letter distressed or rough-edged and so forth.

"Then, if the lettering is to be drawn or done with the broad-edged pen, I fine tune it with several tracing sketches prior to doing a finish. However, if it is a spontaneous script, I write out the word(s) over and over again before choosing the best one or creating the best one from several. (Spontaneity takes a lot of work!)"

— Paul Shaw

"The process of playing with an idea is important in either clarifying the intent of the piece or in creating happy accidents. The subtle nuances of line and what they convey sometimes entails making many, many versions of a word, for example, and then stepping back to evaluate which version contains all the meaning and the technical aspects that I am looking for. Sometimes when I am using this process, I almost want to shut off my conscious mind and let my hand create its own expression. The less analytical interference, the better. I usually try several different types of paper and if using a brush, I may try

John Stevens displays great freedom in this experimental script. The combination of the sweeping bold white strokes with the textured background creates a vibrant, arresting image that could only be achieved through the employment of the free hand.

several different brushes as well. When using a broad-edged pen, I usually already know what line width the piece will require, so I tend to not experiment with that as much. Many times, I will create the expressive quality that I am after, yet I am not satisfied with the technical crafting of what I consider to be a pleasing letterform. In this case I may try to remember and recapture the expressive quality of the line with more careful attention to the technique. This does not always work for me. Sometimes when that inexpressible energy of the hand is impossible to recreate, I will attempt to retouch the original to meet my technical standards. However, I also have decided to go with the expressive version, 'warts and all,' because what it communicates is more important."
 – Joey Hannaford

"First, using thumbnail sketches and doing hands-on calligraphy – fusing together related or unrelated things – helps me to find, hopefully, that arresting image that quietly causes a viewer to stop and look."
 – Terry Louie

"Legibility balanced with expressiveness, stability in style. For example, stocky, heavier weight sans serif is more masculine, expressing industry, machinery, etc. — contrasted with the elegance of a lighter weight script approach. Also, the austere beauty of formal script balanced with the spontaneous, easy-going, modern or trendy 'casual'."
 — Anthony Bloch

It is apparent that for each of these artists, *experimentation* is both intense and very important. Their responses let us know where the true heart of the artisit lies.

Actualization is the final no-nonsense stage of the process. It can be either a difficult or a relatively easy stage depending on the refinement necessary to the earlier experimentation. Jane Dill says, "Too often when working with designers, this is the stage that the calligraphy can be refined to death. I once asked an art director who was telling me to 'make it thicker, etc.' if I could just take it out to a field and shoot it." Nancy Culmone responds, "This can be a very brief 'touch up' or cleaning up of a solution or a very involved piecing together, subtly altering edges, etc., a very meticulous drawing/rendering process with endless 'noodling' of miniscule details."

This piece of art allows the free hand to serve both as illustration and graphics. By combining letter forms and his own unique drawing style into a single unit, Frank Riccio developed this work for the Cleo Society of Trinity College.

Georgia Deaver adds, "In general, I touch up the finished artwork as little as possible, hoping to retain its fresh quality."

John Stevens remarks, "This is usually the easiest or hardest part depending on how far I've pushed and/or how close my preliminary work has brought me to the finish. Remember, calligraphy can be spontaneous. Difficulty can come trying to have too many criteria for one piece or solution, resulting in one canceling out the other.

This is the *committee zone.*"

Their words reflect the awareness that whatever comes from this last stage, no matter what transpired before, that is how their work will be seen by the public in the marketplace. This will be what will be judged. Marsha Brady says, "Generally what appeals to me and what I feel I can actually 'pull off' with the same 'feeling' that came about in the initial experimenting stage may be the thing that decides the direction — as long as it is right for the mood I want to get."

This is the stage where everything comes to bear on the final art. All the previous stages influence the decisions, and their combination and distillation will be the end product. Larry Brady responds, "In the process of giving full reign to the tools in the hand, and the exploration of many ideas and many directions, one is able to arrive at the combination of tools, techniques, and ideas that will provide the most original yet good answer to a design problem. The freehand approach remains a major force with its inexhaustable variety of creations unique and excellent."

Another extremely important issue when considering the final execution is mentioned by Sherry Bringham. "Critical to the success of the piece is a full understanding of the printing process and using it to one's best advantage." Nothing could be more disasterous than an image that cannot be translated to the printed page.

This article has been a partial journey through the experiences of some highly acclaimed artists and is only a brief look at this creative process. Much more could be said and many more avenues in the process could be opened up, but in the end it seems to come down to preparation, skill, and freedom. Thus, Colleen says, "It seems to me the reasons for solutions are based on some magic combination of one's learned and innate abilities."

From the collection of Carolyn Baldwin

Displaying this untitled piece of fine art by Marsha Brady is a perfect way to close this article on viability. The use of the suggested letterform to show color, direction, and form is beautifully presented here, and would be equally successful if it found its stylistic way into the world of applied commercial graphics.

The Art

Speaks for Itself

The following 141 pages contain examples
of applied design work that clearly demonstrate the uniqueness and flexibility of
freehand graphics. The artists shown here
have an adaptability that transcends the
usual range of expression both in style and
content. They are not restrained by convention or personal style, and they reach out
in diverse directions to gain appropriate
results. This is truly a visual treasure chest
of successful design work utilizing what is
surely the most fundamental of all design
tools: the free hand.

Paul Shaw

The work of this New York based artist underscores the idea of versatility. It ranges from the classic to the playful. It sometimes serves as the dominant element and sometimes as the supportive carrier of the message. The pieces displayed on these two pages and pages 24–25 show how well his art works within each completed design. The images shown on pages 22–23 give an indication of the range of his freehand styles.

Design Firm: Staff
Art Director: Carl Grifassi
Designer: Carl Grifassi
Client: Lord & Taylor

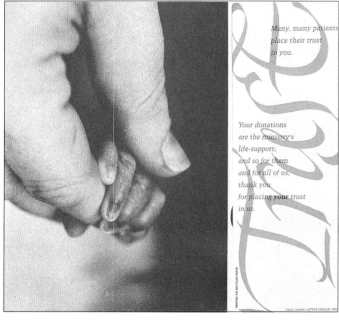

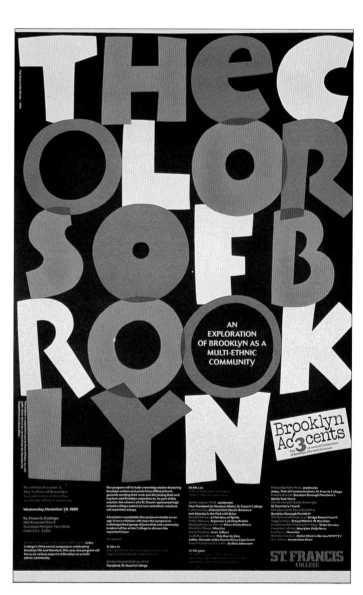

Art Director: Paul Shaw
Designer: Paul Shaw
Illustrator: Marian Parry
Client: Paul Shaw & Marian Parry

Design Firm: Paul Shaw/Letter Design
Art Director: Paul Shaw
Designer: Paul Shaw
Client: St. Francis College

Design Firm: Paul Shaw/Letter Design
Art Director: Paul Shaw
Designer: Paul Shaw
Client: The Methodist Hospital

Design Firm: Staff
Art Director: Susan Black
Designer: Jenifer Cohen
Calligrapher: Paul Shaw
Client: Lord & Taylor

Design Firm: Staff
Art Director: Gary Sitomer
Designer: Brenda Miller
Calligrapher: Paul Shaw
Client: Clairol

Design Firm: Nelson Kane
Art Director: Nelson Kane
Designer: Nelson Kane
Calligrapher: Paul Shaw
Client: *Weavings*

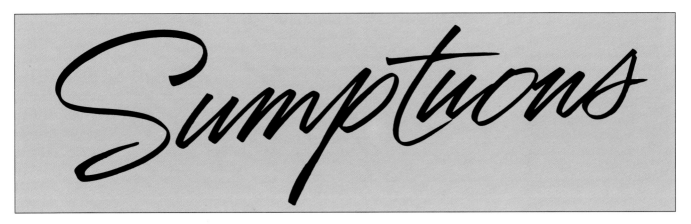

Design Firm: Staff
Art Director: Susan Black
Designer: Susan Black
Calligrapher: Paul Shaw
Client: Lord & Taylor

Design Firm: Staff
Art Director: Scott Fishoff
Designer: Joan Piekny
Calligrapher: Paul Shaw
Client: Clairol

Design Firm: Staff
Art Director: Scott Fishoff
Designer: YJ Lee
Calligrapher: Paul Shaw
Client: Clairol

Design Firm: Rudi Wolff Design
Art Director: Rudy Wolff
Designer: Rudy Wolff
Calligrapher: Paul Shaw
Client: Deloitte Touche

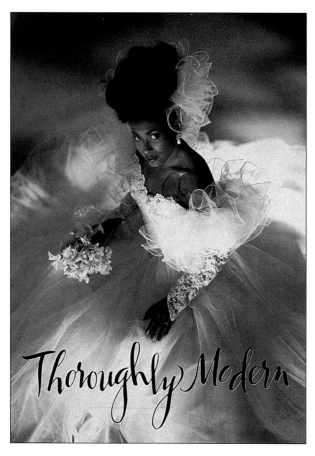

Design Firm: Staff
Art Director: Debra Gill
Designer: Debra Gill
Client: *Modern Bride*

Design Firm: Staff
Art Director: Iris Magidson
Designer: Sara Hendelman
Client: Clairol

Design Firm: Staff
Art Director: Scott Fishoff
Designer: Joan Piekny
Client: Clairol

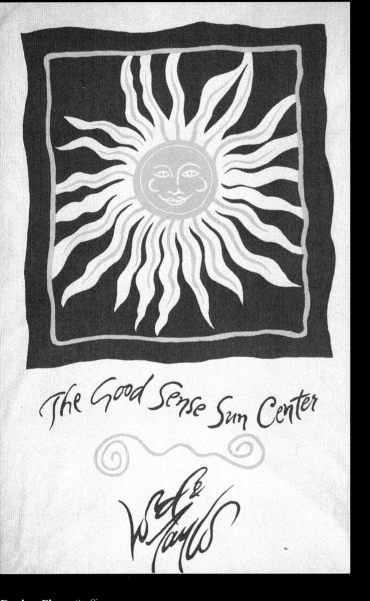

Emmy Award-winning actress Alfre Woodard portrays Andrea Crawford, a lady who has worked hard to rise from the black ghetto to become a top advertising executive. Her work is her life until one day she meets, quite by chance, Jackie Watson—a cute, self-sufficient 7-year-old who is selling drugs on a New York City street.

Taken aback by this youngster's lifestyle, Andrea discovers in Jackie a highly intelligent child with a gift for flights of fancy that border on the poetic. But breaking through to this elusive street kid means searching through rough ghetto streets—and a face-off with the pusher who controls the boy's life. But Andrea's determination pays off as she and Jackie head off to start a new life together in California.

Design Firm: Staff
Art Director: Joel Azzerad
Designer: Joel Azzerad
Client: NBC

Design Firm: Staff
Art Director: Susan Black
Designer: Jennifer Cohen
Illustrator: Jennifer Cohen

Colleen

In the pieces displayed on the next six pages, Colleen, who works out of Brookline, Massachusetts, shows how well she integrates her work with whatever the accompanying art. Whether it be the light-line quietness of "Still Light," created for Monadnock Paper Mills, or the playful almost childlike caption on the carrying bag, created for Houghton Mifflin Company, there is a real relationship between the letterforms and the design. The book cover, "The Resourceful Writer," also created for Houghton Mifflin Company, is an excellent use of color and the free hand to establish the letterforms as the only art necessary for this strong design.

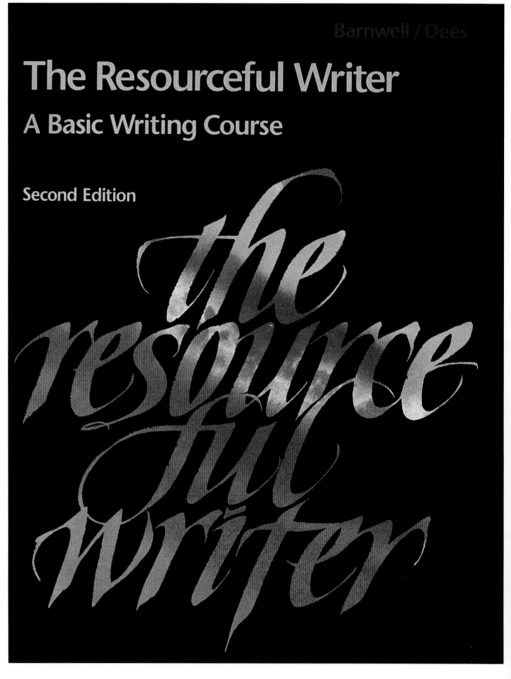

Designer: Mark Caleb
Client: Houghton Mifflin Company

Design Firm: Rob MacIntosh Communications
Designer: Rob MacIntosh
Client: Monadnock Paper Mills, Inc.

Art Director/Designer: Diana Helm
Client: Houghton Mifflin Company

Design Firm: Arnold & Company
Designer: Linda Lampman
Client: Fleet Bank

Designer: Laurie Boyden
Client: Data Net

Hear the Difference

" When our lives get too hectic, we go to
an H&H concert and the sheer quality of
the experience renews and enriches us. "

— **Barbara Cotta, H&H subscriber since 1987**

3

Hear the Difference

" When our lives get too hectic, we go to
an H&H concert and the sheer quality of
the experience renews and enriches us. "

— **Barbara Cotta, H&H subscriber since 1987**

3

Design Firm: Komarow Design
Designer: Ronnie Komarow
Client: Handel & Haydn Society

Designer: Julianna Horton
Artwork: from the collection of The Museum of Fine Arts, Boston
Client: The Museum of Fine Arts, Boston

Designer: Diana Parziale
Photographer: Jon Jones
Client: Boston University

Bruce MacCombie
Dean, School for the Arts

Wilbur D. Fullbright
Director of Music

Superb musical training in Boston, internationally recognized as one of the most exciting cultural and historical centers in the world.

Auditions in Boston and selected regional sites.

**BOSTON
UNIVERSITY
TANGLEWOOD
INSTITUTE**

Intensive summer programs in the Berkshire Hills offered for college credit in conjunction with the Boston Symphony Orchestra.

One of the greatest thrills among a series of memorable ones was conducting a rehearsal of the Boston University Tanglewood Young Artists Orchestra. The eagerness and joy with which they absorbed every musical moment gave me great gratification and hope for America's youth.
 ~ Leonard Bernstein

Write:
Boston University
School for the Arts/Music
855 Commonwealth Avenue
Room 264
Boston, MA 02215
Or phone toll free:
1-800-643-4796

**BOSTON
UNIVERSITY**

Illustrator: Colleen
Client: Anita Hill (owner)

Sherry Bringham

Sherry Bringham of El Cerrito, California, has a real talent for bold direct calligraphy. All of her pieces shown here indicate a boldness in style even when the script is refined. When comparing the broad stroke of "The Legend Comes to Life" to the more delicate but equally eye-catching script of her "Wildest Dreams" Christmas card, you can't help but sense the impact of her work. These examples and all those on pages 32–37 are living proof that emphasis and impact can be created through many different styles and freehand interpretations.

Design Firm: Pinné Herbers
Designer: Linda Clark
Client: Mandarin Hotel

Design Firm: B & B Associates
Designer: Sherry Bringham
Client: B & B Associates

Design Firm: Salthouse Torre Norton, Inc.
Designer: David Recchia
Client: Napa Valley

Design Firm: Axion Design
Designer: Jack Wright
Client: Schilling

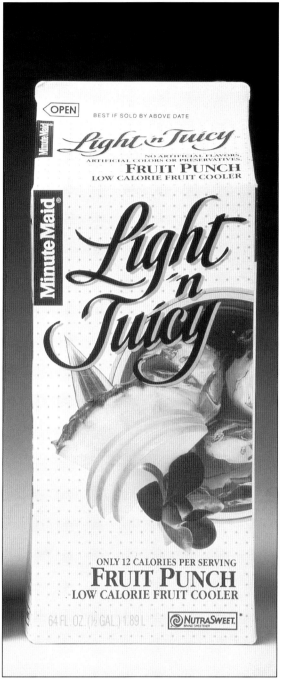

Design Firm: Landor & Associates
Designer: Margo Zucker
Client: Weitek

Design Firm: Axion Design
Designer: Lisa Brussel
Client: Minute Maid

Design Firm: Ogilvy & Mather Direct
Designer: Beverly Adler
Client: Forbes Magazine

Design Firm: The Ram Group
Designer: Sandy Cooper
Client: Charles Krug Winery (Seagrams)

The Spice of Life

Design Firm: Gronet Design
Designer: Susanne Holm
Client: Fetzer Vineyards

Design Firm: Foote Cone & Belding
Designer: Dave Dembowski
Client: Taco Bell

Design Firm: Arnold Fortuna Lawner & Cabot Advertising, Inc.
Designer: Jennifer Tisdale
Client: Kinney Shoes

John Sayles

This designer/artist from Des Moines has a unique and colorful approach to freehand graphics. Using a strong primary sense of color, frequently applied in broad strokes, he creates dramatic and arresting graphics that quickly command the viewer's attention. Good examples of this are the promotional package for The Studio Group, which includes a T-shirt and custom box, and the commemorative poster for CT Corporation which has a calligraphic feeling without incorporating any actual letterforms.

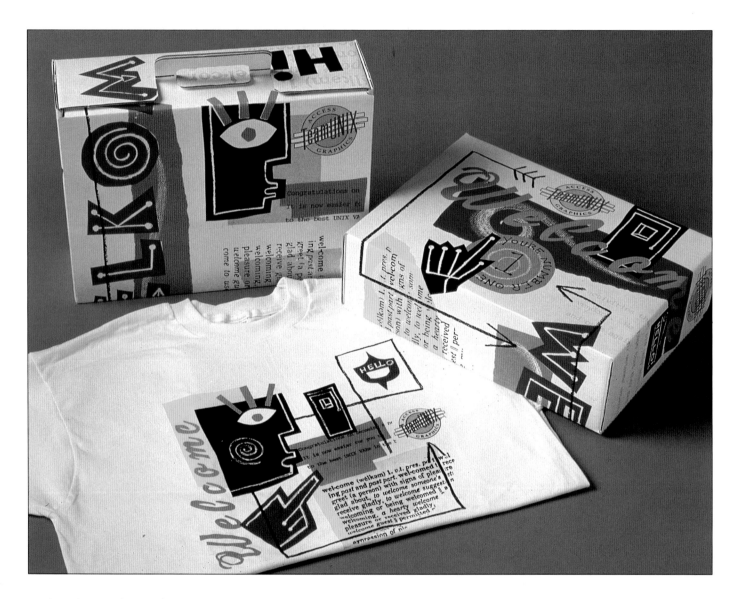

Design Firm: Sayles Graphic Design
Art Director: John Sayles
Designer: John Sayles
Illustrator: John Sayles
Client: The Studio Group

Design Firm: Sayles Graphic Design
Art Director: John Sayles
Designer: John Sayles
Illustrator: John Sayles
Client: CT Corporation

Design Firm: Sayles Graphic Design
Art Director: John Sayles
Designer: John Sayles
Illustrator: John Sayles
Client: Warner Books

Design Firm: Sayles Graphic Design
Art Director: John Sayles
Designer: John Sayles
Illustrator: John Sayles
Client: Villanova University

Design Firm: Sayles Graphic Design
Art Director: John Sayles
Designer: John Sayles
Illustrator: John Sayles
Client: Beckley Imports

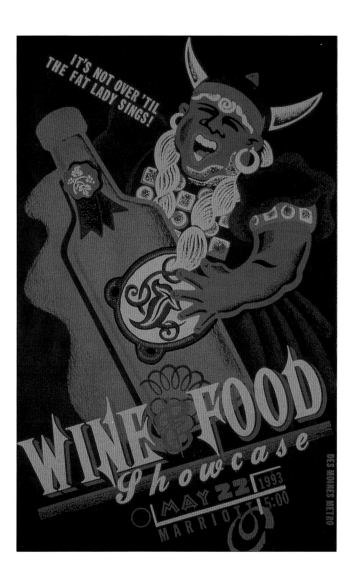

Design Firm: Sayles Graphic Design
Art Director: John Sayles
Designer: John Sayles
Illustrator: John Sayles
Client: Des Moines Metropolitan Opera

Design Firm: Sayles Graphic Design
Art Director: John Sayles
Designer: John Sayles
Illustrator: John Sayles
Client: Hyatt Newporter

Design Firm: Sayles Graphic Design
Art Director: John Sayles
Designer: John Sayles
Illustrator: John Sayles
Client: Central Life Assurance

Design Firm: Sayles Graphic Design
Art Director: John Sayles
Designer: John Sayles
Illustrator: John Sayles
Client: The Boys & Girls Club of Central Iowa

Design Firm: Sayles Graphic Design
Art Director: John Sayles
Designer: John Sayles
Illustrator: John Sayles
Client: 801 Steak & Chop House

Design Firm: Sayles Graphic Design
Art Director: John Sayles
Designer: John Sayles
Illustrator: John Sayles
Client: 801 Steak & Chop House

Edward Vartanian

Working out of Cranston, Rhode Island, Eddie Vartanian has long embraced the visceral component in his work. He believes the "mark" has a voice that comes from the "...tactile exploration of form and space." An interesting and unusual example is the logo for the movie "Sharkey's Machine." Once the idea of neon lights had suggested itself, the typography was hand drawn and shot in separate stages — line, underglow, and in-line burn, producing an excellent example of what can be done with creative control of technology.

Design Firm: Diener Hauser and Bates, Los Angeles
Art Director: Vincent Aniano, Edward Vartanian
Illustrator: Edward Vartanian
Client: Burt Reynolds Productions

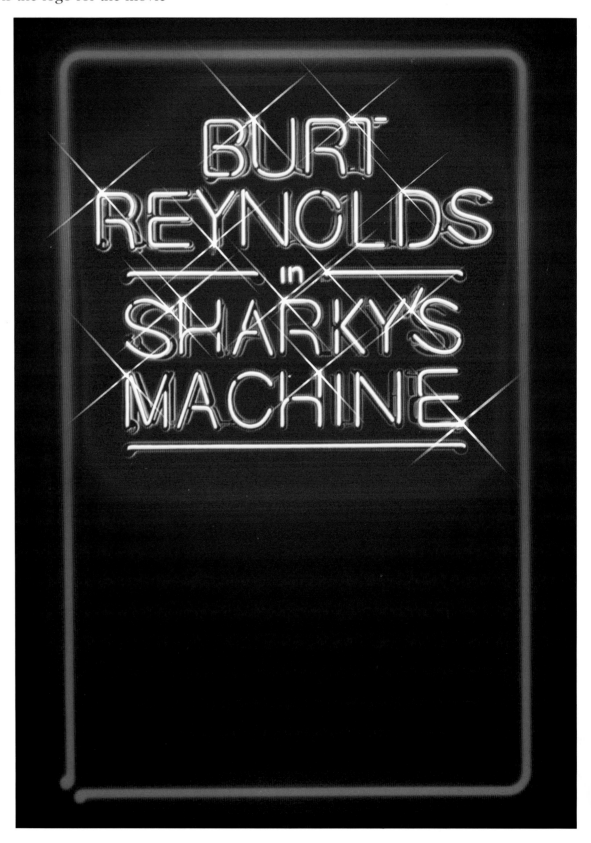

Design Firm: Vartanian Design
Art Director: Tom Williams
Illustrator: Edward Vartanian
Client: CBS

Design Firm: Lubalin Associates
Art Director: Herb Lubalin
Illustrator: Edward Vartanian
Client: Playboy

Design Firm: Vartanian Design
Art Director: Jerry Counihan
Illustrator: Edward Vartanian
Client: Loveline Books

Design Firm: Vartanian Design
Art Director: Jerry Pfiefer
Illustrator: Edward Vartanian
Client: Bantam Books

Design Firm: Vartanian Design
Art Director: Edward Vartanian
Illustrator: Edward Vartanian
Client: The Potting Shed Restaurant

Design Firm: Vartanian Design
Art Director: Edward Vartanian
Illustrator: Edward Vartanian
Client: The Little Symphony

Julian Waters

As can be seen in the examples shown on pages 48-53, Julian Waters' work finds its way into many different forms of reproduction. It has been embossed (below), it has been engraved on glass (opposite), and it has appeared on postage stamps (page 50). The remaining pieces show his unique and creative interpretation of the various letter forms as they combine with art and photography to make beautiful finished expressions.

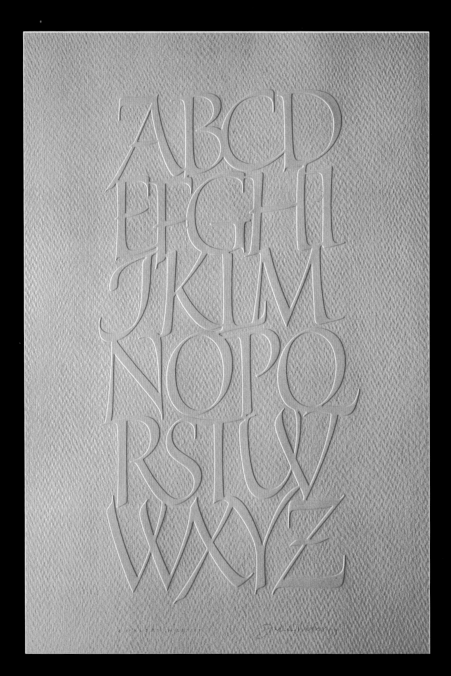

Design Firm: Julian Waters
Art Director: Julian Waters

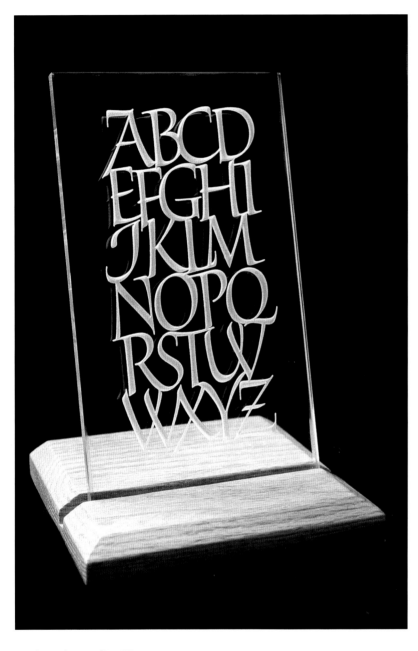

Design Firm: Julian Waters
Art Directors: Julian Waters, David Pankow
Illustrator: Julian Waters
Client: Rochester Institute of Technology

Design Firm: The Kamber Group
Art Director: Karen Thompson
Illustrator: Julian Waters
Client: Corporation for Public Broadcasting

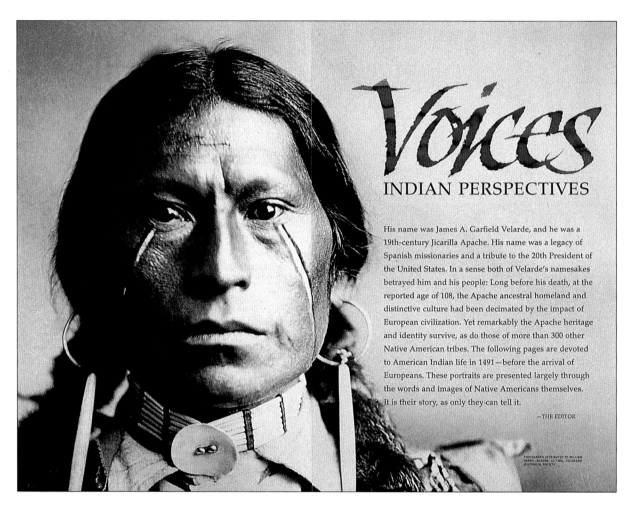

Voices
INDIAN PERSPECTIVES

His name was James A. Garfield Velarde, and he was a 19th-century Jicarilla Apache. His name was a legacy of Spanish missionaries and a tribute to the 20th President of the United States. In a sense both of Velarde's namesakes betrayed him and his people: Long before his death, at the reported age of 108, the Apache ancestral homeland and distinctive culture had been decimated by the impact of European civilization. Yet remarkably the Apache heritage and identity survive, as do those of more than 300 other Native American tribes. The following pages are devoted to American Indian life in 1491—before the arrival of Europeans. These portraits are presented largely through the words and images of Native Americans themselves. It is their story, as only they can tell it.

—THE EDITOR

PHOTOGRAPH ATTRIBUTED TO WILLIAM HENRY JACKSON, CA 1900, COLORADO HISTORICAL SOCIETY

Design Firm: National Geographic Society
Art Directors: Constance Phelps/Allen Carroll
Calligrapher: Julian Waters
Client: *National Geographic*

Design Firm: Lou Nolan
Art Director: Perry Noyes Craig
Illustrators: Lou Nolan/Julian Waters
Client: U.S. Postal Service

Design Firm: Picture Book Studio
Art Director: Robert Saunders
Illustrator: David Scott Meier
Client: Picture Book Studio

Design Firm: Picture Book Studio
Art Director: Robert Saunders
Illustrator: Ivan Gantschev
Client: Picture Book Studio

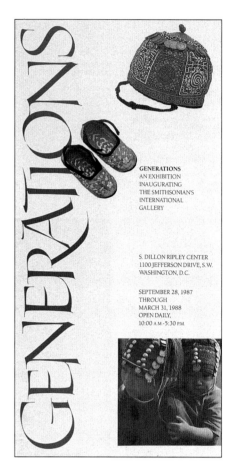

Design Firm: Cathy & Julian Waters
Art Director: Cathy & Julian Waters
Illustrator: Cathy Waters
Client: GEIST musical group

Design Firm: GrafikCommunications, Inc.
Art Director: Judy Kirpich
Calligrapher: Julian Waters
Client: Smithsonian Institution

Design Firm: National Geographic Society
Art Director: Gerry Valesio
Calligrapher: Julian Waters
Client: *National Geographic*

Design Firm: National Geographic Society
Art Director: Gerry Valerio
Calligrapher: Julian Waters
Client: *National Geographic*

Design Firm: Julian Waters
Art Directors: Julian Waters/Tony Futch
Photographer: Gary Landsman
Client: S&S Graphics, Inc.

Jane Dill

One of the strengths of Jane Dill as a calligrapher is her attention to classic form. No matter how delightfully outrageous or clearly traditional her efforts may be they never lose their connection to real letterforms and typographical tradition. Her "Caritas" calendar page is a perfect example of this. The film title "Guardianes del Futuro," done for a documentary about the Lacandon Maya (rainforest people of Southern Mexico) also gives a feeling of the subject matter while retaining real letter form.

Designer: Bill Zemanek
Stylist: Jan Rhodes
Photographer: Bill Zemanek
Client: American Heart Association

Calligrapher/Art Director: Jane Dill
Producers: Jaime Kibben, Steve Bartz
Client: Conservation International

Designer/Calligrapher: Jane Dill
Mac Assistance: Stephen Brusewitz

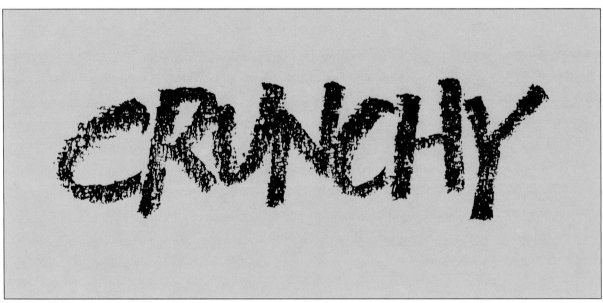

(top)
Design Firm: Macropolis
Art Director: Stephen Brusewitz
Calligrapher: Jane Dill
Client: Albanese Hair Design

(bottom)
Design Firm: SBG Partners
Art Director: Kate Greene
Calligrapher: Jane Dill
Client: Cheetos (Frito Lay)

Design Firm: SBG Partners, San Francisco
Art Director: Kate Greene
Client: Cole's Baking Company

Design Firm: Landor Associates, San Francisco
Art Director: Michael Livolsi
Client: Seagram's Beverage Company

Designer: Barbara Szerlip
Art Direction: Barbara Szerlip, Jane Dill
Client: Pomegranate Publications

Calligraphy/Design: Jane Dill
Client: Tom Richardson
High Score Music

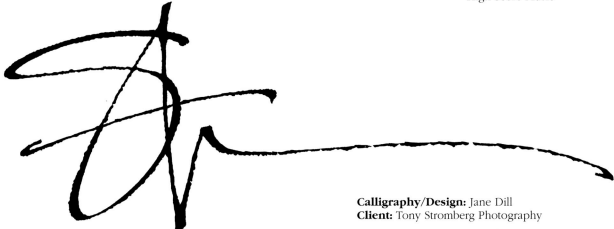

Calligraphy/Design: Jane Dill
Client: Tony Stromberg Photography

Design/Lettering: Jane Dill
(with inspiration by Karlgeorg Hoeffer)
Typography: Kirk Fetzer, Fetzer Design,
San Francisco

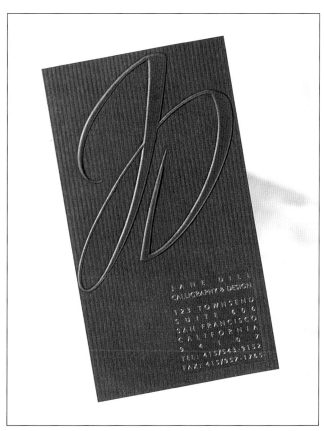

Terry Louie

The quality that is most significant in the work of Terry Louie is his subtlety. This is evident in the pieces displayed on the next four pages, whether he is the calligrapher himself or the designer that employs the art of others. In his own work an Oriental influence permeates. Terry is art director and editor of the magazine *Alphabet, The Journal of the Friends of Calligraphy*. The first two pages are examples of his cover design for that publication, and the following pages are some inside spread designs and other commercial pieces.

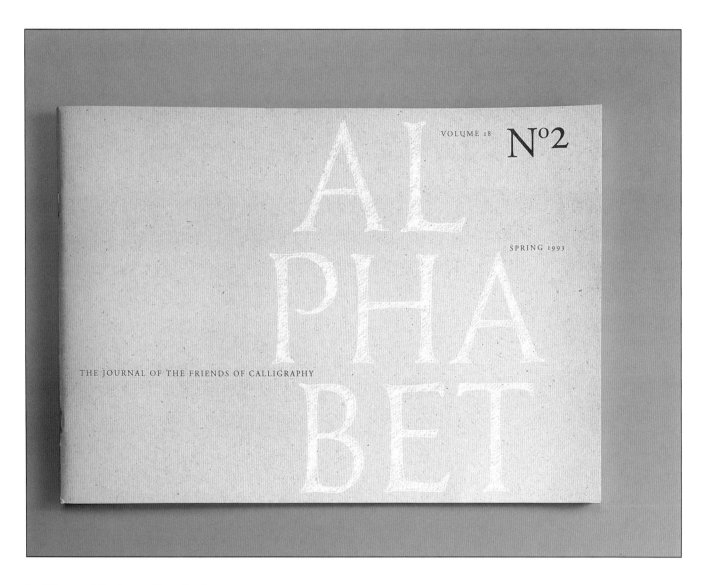

Art Director/ Designer: Terry Louie
Calligrapher: Kathy McNicholas
Client: Alphabet

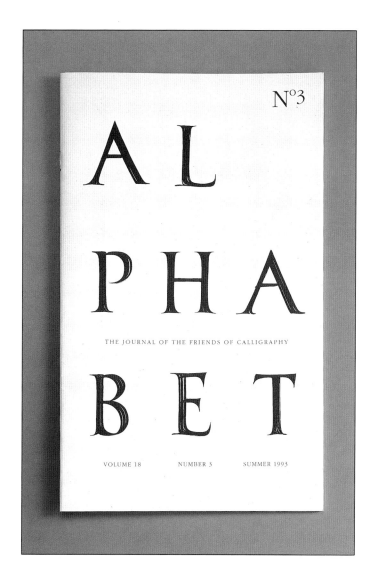

Art Director/Designer: Terry Louie
Calligrapher: Claude Deiterich A.
Client: *Alphabet*

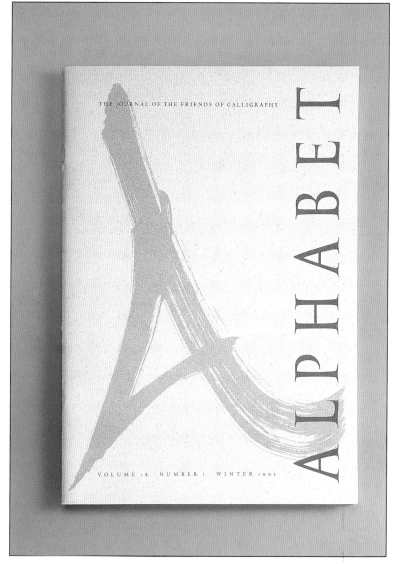

Art Director/Designer: Terry Louie
Calligrapher: Terry Louie
Typographer: Mark van Bronkhorst
Client: *Alphabet*

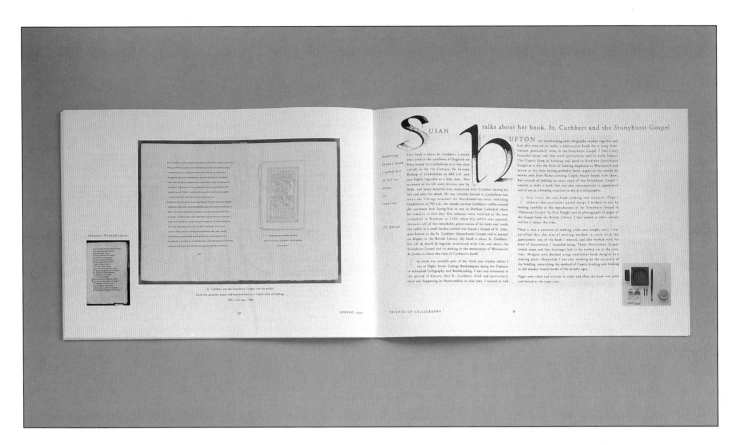

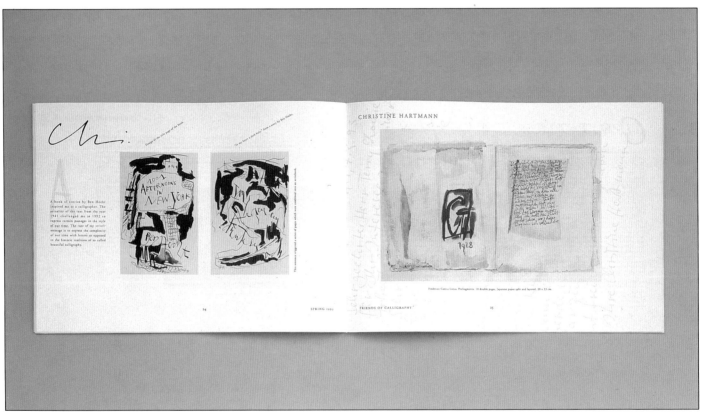

Art Director/Designer: Terry Louie
Calligrapher: Terry Louie
Client: *Alphabet*

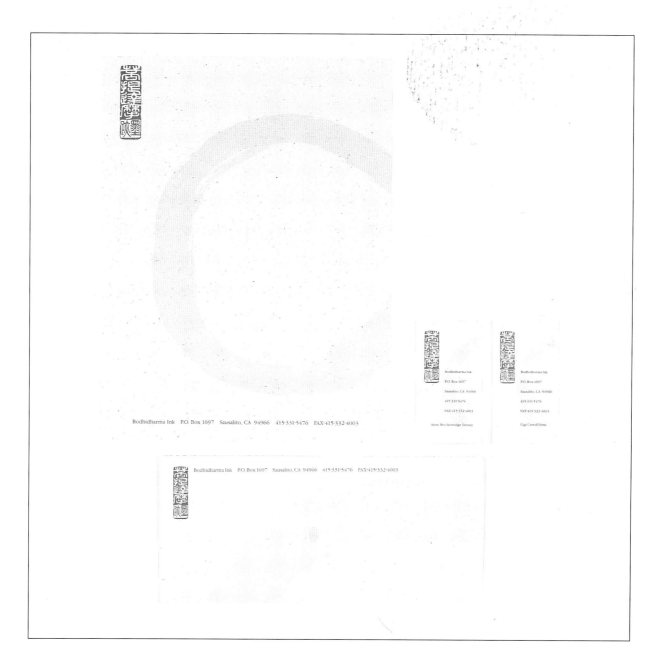

Art Director/Designer: Terry Louie
Seal Design: Terry Louie
Seal Engraving: Shen Huiwei
Client: Bodhidharma Ink

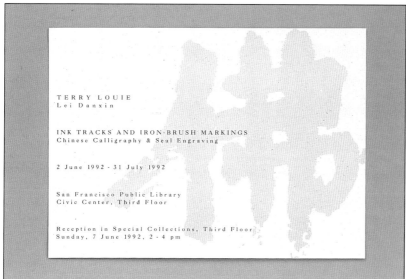

Art Director/Calligrapher: Terry Louie
Designer: Terry Louie
Client: Self-promotion

Mike Quon

Mike Quon has a unique talent for introducing the freehand brush stroke to his graphics. The next four pages display examples of an illustrative style that, because it is reduced to just a few strokes, becomes graphic design that has a Far Eastern quality. Whether he is putting his mark on posters, advertising, or T-shirts, he produces the same bright primary-color design.

Design Firm: Mike Quon Design Office
Art Directors: Scott Fishoff, Mike Quon
Designer: Mike Quon
Illustrator: Mike Quon
Client: Clairol

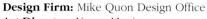

Design Firm: Mike Quon Design Office
Art Director: Nancy Martino
Designer: Mike Quon
Illustrator: Mike Quon
Client: Meadox

Design Firm: Mike Quon Design Office
Art Director: Michael Connelly
Designer: Mike Quon
Illustrator: Mike Quon
Client: Warner Music

Design Firm: Mike Quon Design Office
Art Director: Nancy Martino
Designer: Mike Quon
Illustrator: Mike Quon
Client: Meadox/Stylus

Design Firm: Mike Quon Design Office
Art Director: Scott Fishoff, Mike Quon
Designer: Mike Quon
Illustrator: Mike Quon
Client: Clairol

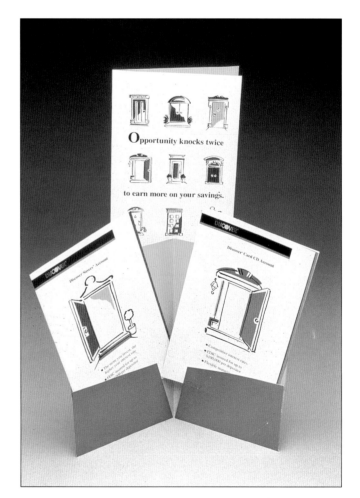

Design Firm: Mike Quon Design Office
Art Director: Mike Quon
Designer: Mike Quon
Illustrator: Mike Quon
Client: Discover Card

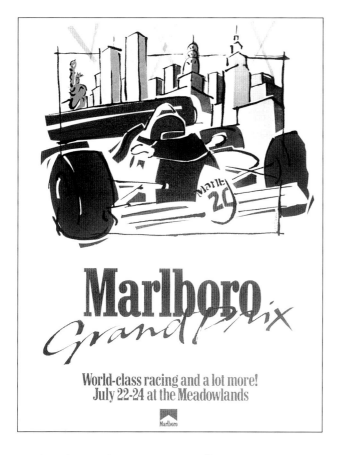

Design Firm: Mike Quon Design Office
Art Director: Mike Quon
Designer: Mike Quon
Illustrator: Mike Quon
Client: Marlboro

Design Firm: Mike Quon Design Office
Art Director: Domingo Perez
Designer: Mike Quon
Illustrator: Mike Quon
Client: Cutex

Design Firm: Mike Quon Design Office
Art Director: Gro Frivoll
Designer: Mike Quon
Illustrator: Mike Quon
Client: The American Museum of Natural History

Daniel Riley

A strong sense of commercial application is in the work of Dan Riley. He knows how to use the freehand stroke to its best advantage whether it be with logos or in package design. Each of the pieces shown on the next six pages shows this consistency as well as his ability to convey a strong sense of freedom without losing legibility.

Design Firm: Riley Design Associates
Art Director: Daniel Riley
Designer: Daniel Riley
Illustrator: Daniel Riley
Client: On Silk (Identity)

Design Firm: Riley Design Associates
Art Director: Daniel Riley
Designer: Daniel Riley
Illustrator: Daniel Riley
Client: El Camino Grooming

Design Firm: Riley Design Associates
Art Director: Daniel Riley
Designer: Daniel Riley
Illustrator: Daniel Riley
Client: Self-promotion

Design Firm: Riley Design Associates
Art Director: Daniel Riley
Designer: Daniel Riley
Illustrator: Daniel Riley
Client: Lobob Laboratories, Inc.

Design Firm: Riley Design Associates
Art Director: Daniel Riley
Designer: Daniel Riley
Illustrator: Daniel Riley
Client: Berndes

Design Firm: Riley Design Associates
Art Director: Daniel Riley
Designer: Daniel Riley
Illustrator: Daniel Riley
Client: Beau Monde

BEAU MONDE
FINE FLOOR COVERINGS

DISTRIBUTORS

Design Firm: Riley Design Associates
Art Director: Daniel Riley
Designer: Daniel Riley
Illustrator: Daniel Riley
Client: Chez Distributors

Design Firm: Riley Design Associates
Art Director: Daniel Riley
Designer: Daniel Riley
Illustrator: Daniel Riley
Client: San Mateo Executive Club

Design Firm: Riley Design Associates
Art Director: Daniel Riley
Designer: Daniel Riley
Illustrator: Daniel Riley
Client: American Management Systems

Design Firm: Riley Design Associates
Art Director: Daniel Riley
Designer: Daniel Riley
Illustrator: Daniel Riley
Client: Train, Inc.

TRAINING ■ RESOURCE AND
INFORMATION NETWORK, INC.

Design Firm: Riley Design Associates
Art Director: Daniel Riley
Designer: Daniel Riley
Illustrator: Daniel Riley
Client: Boy Oh Boy Productions

Design Firm: Riley Design Associates
Art Director: Daniel Riley
Designer: Daniel Riley
Illustrator: Daniel Riley
Client: Paint Box

Design Firm: Riley Design Associates
Art Director: Daniel Riley
Designer: Daniel Riley
Illustrator: Daniel Riley
Client: San Francisco Softball Team

Jean Evans

Jean Evans has successfully incorporated her love of fine art calligraphy in her commercial work. As can be seen on these pages, she has produced a wide range of applications from book covers to labels and packaging. Especially interesting was her commission in 1992 by jazz aficionados Joan and Rod Nordell to create an artist book based on the handwriting of trumpeter Dizzy Gillespie to celebrate his 75th birthday (page 77). The text of this book, *Dizzy opus ii*, was based on a conversation Jean had with him in 1991, and the typeface was her own digitilization of his handwriting.

Designer: Deborah Brown
Calligrapher: Jean Evans
Client: Boston University

Design Firm: Milhon Design
Designer: Marjorie Milhon
Calligrapher: Jean Evans
Client: Chad Farm, a New Zealand
Vineyard

Design Firm: Milhon Design
Designer: Marjorie Milhon
Calligrapher: Jean Evans
Client: Harpoon Ale, Boston Brewery

Calligrapher: Jean Evans

SCHUMANN
Designer/Art director: Janice Wheeler
Client: Northeastern University Press

SOPHISTICATED REBELS
Designer/Art director: Gwen Frankfeld
Client: Harvard University Press

SOR JUANA
Designer/Art director: Amy Berstein
Client: Harvard University Press

Design Firm: Maynard/Tragakis Design
Designer: Mary Anne Tragakis
Calligrapher: Jean Evans
Client: C'est la Vie, Marblehead, MA

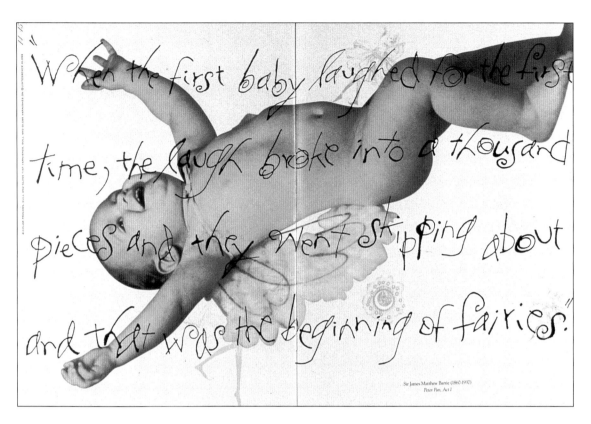

When the first baby laughed for the first time, the laugh broke into a thousand pieces and they went skipping about and that was the beginning of fairies."

Sir James Matthew Barrie (1860-1937)
Peter Pan, Act I

Design Firm: The Kuester Group, Minneapolis
Designer: Brent Marmo
Calligrapher: Jean Evans
Client: Potlatch Paper Company

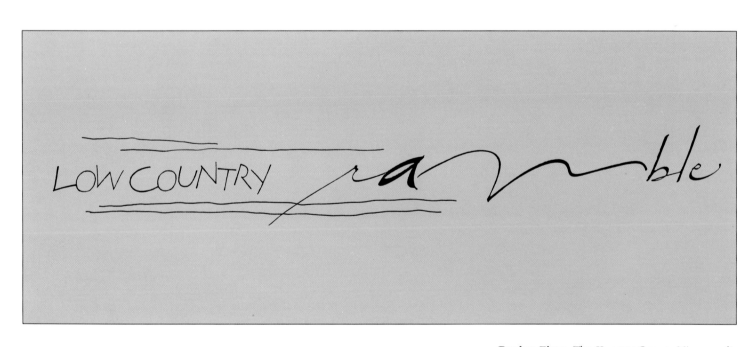

LOW COUNTRY ramble

Design Firm: The Kuester Group, Minneapolis
Designer: Brent Marmo
Calligrapher: Jean Evans
Client: Infinity

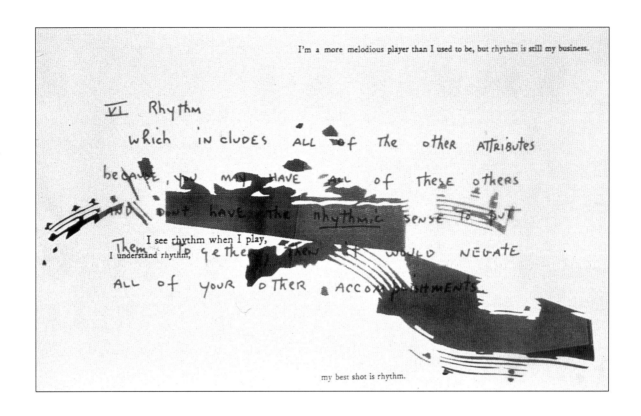

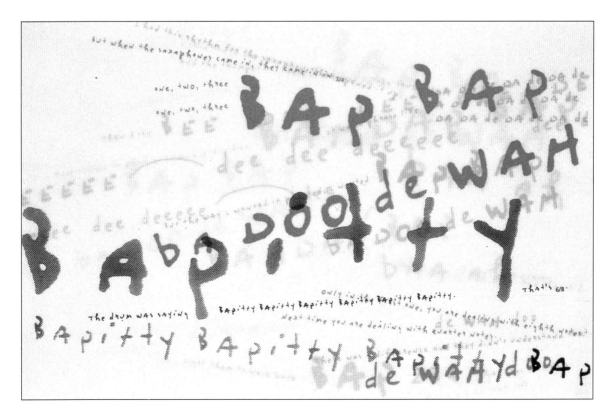

Commission: Joan and Rod Nordell
Designer: Jean Evans
Calligrapher: Jean Evans

Claude Dieterich A.

As can be seen in the examples on pages 78–81, Claude Dieterich A. has a unique flair for script lettering. His natural flourish and spontaneous sweep give great style to his art. On the opposite page are two more of his design pieces for the Argentine magazine, *tipoGráfica* (see page 9). They again show a wonderful use of letterforms in design.

Calligrapher: Claude Dieterich A.
Client: Great Flamenco Singers

Calligrapher: Claude Dieterich A.
Client: The Sleep of Reason

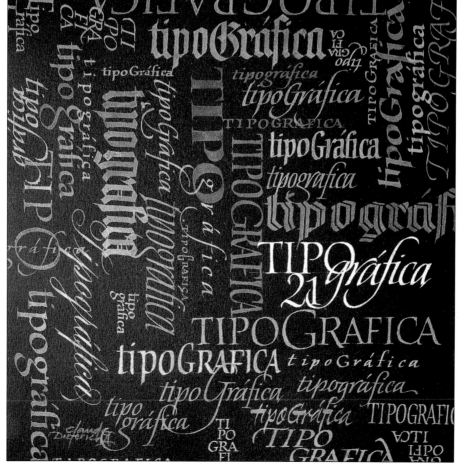

Designer: Claude Dieterich A.
Calligrapher: Claude Dieterich A.
Client: *tipoGráfica*

Calligrapher: Claude Dieterich A.
Client: Academy of Art College,
San Francisco

Calligrapher: Claude Dieterich A.
Client: Sculpture exhibition

Calligrapher: Claude Dieterich A.
Client: Cante Jondo

Calligrapher: Claude Dieterich A.
Client: Latin America Travel

HISPANIC CULTURAL ARTS

Calligrapher: Claude Dieterich A.
Client: Hispanic Cultural Arts

Larry Brady

One of the most important considerations for designing ID spots is adaptability, especially with imaginative freehand. This is one of Larry Brady's strengths, shown on the following two pages as he develops the image for the full range of *Lavosh* products. The strength of the letterforms works beautifully with the different floral patterns and creates a consistent name recognition. The remaining pieces displayed on pages 84–87 show equally the successful relationship between letterforms and art.

Art Director: Larry Brady
Calligrapher: Larry Brady
Illustrator: Larry Brady
Client: Adrienne's Gourmet Foods

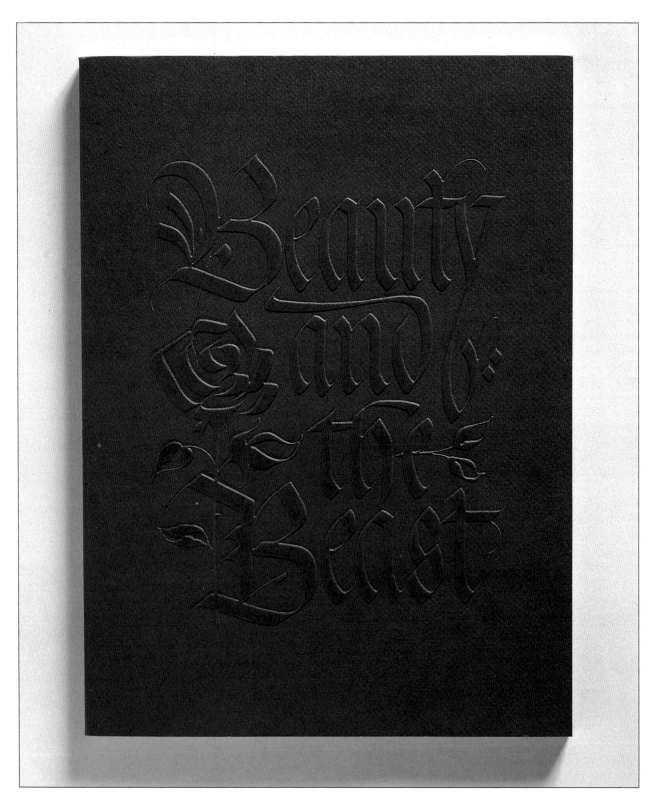

Art Director: Larry Brady
Design: Marsha and Larry Brady
Calligrapher: Marsha Brady
Client: Green Tiger Press

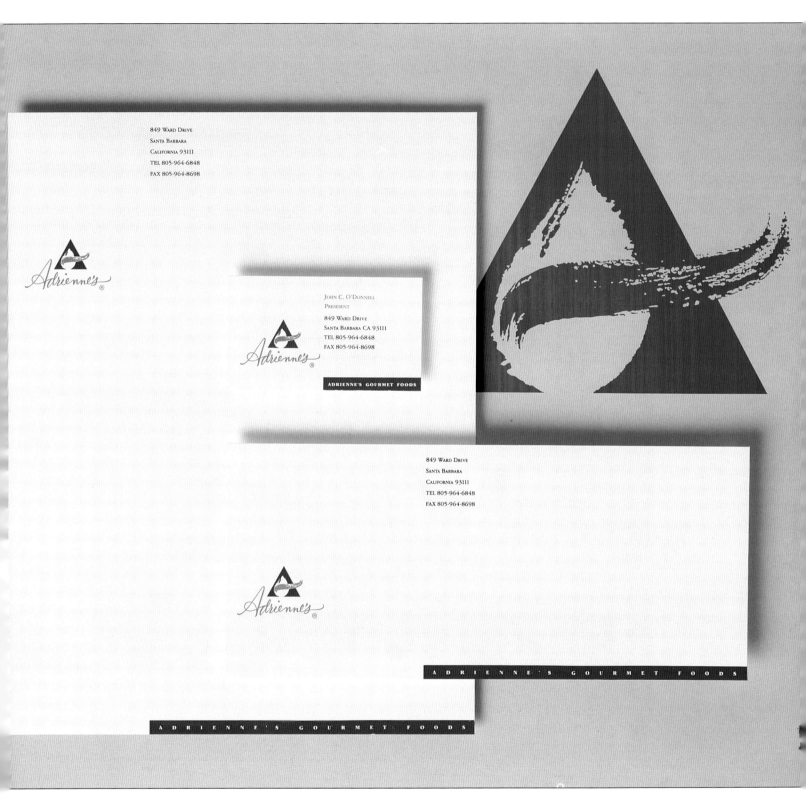

Art Director: Larry Brady
Designers: Bonnie Leah, Larry Brady
Client: Adrienne's Gourmet Foods

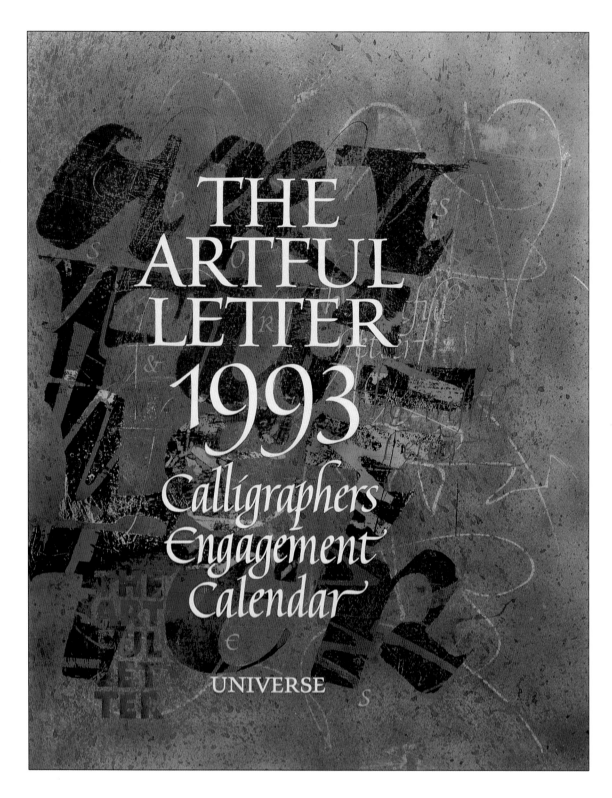

Art Director: Larry Brady
Designer: Larry Brady
Calligrapher: Larry Brady
Client: Universe Publishing

Art Director: Ron Taft
Designer: Larry Brady
Calligrapher: Larry Brady
Client: Ron Taft

The International Worship Resource Network ◆ P.O. Box 31050 ◆ Laguna Hills, CA 92654-1050

Art Director: Larry Brady
Designer: Larry Brady
Calligrapher: Larry Brady
Client: Maranatha Music

Ivan Angelic

The artwork of Ivan Angelic has a strong professional consistency and a deft use of his tools. An excellent example of this is the poster promoting an exhibition of Eastern and Western calligraphy. The art intentionally represents each culture, and the use of color is evocative of the combination of them. The remaining pieces on pages 88–93 continue to illustrate that consistency with other examples.

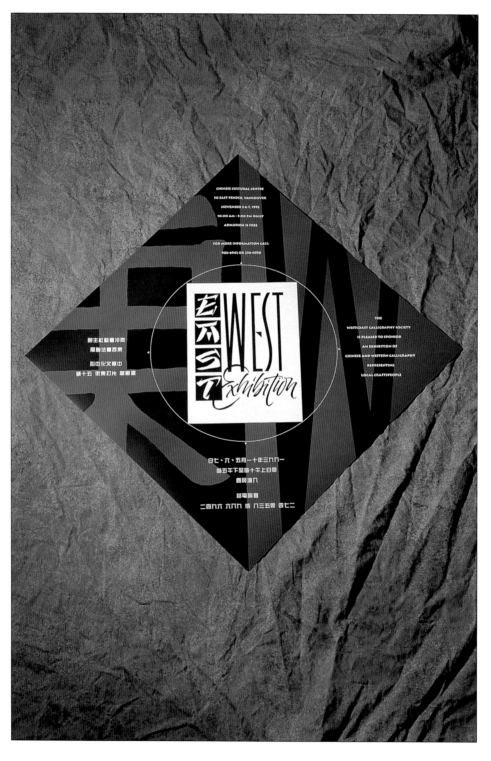

Design Firm: Hoffmann & Angelic Design
Designer: Ivan Angelic
Calligrapher: Ivan Angelic
Client: Westcoast Calligraphy Society

Design Firm: Hoffmann & Angelic Design
Art Director: Andrea Hoffmann
Calligrapher: Ivan Angelic
Illustrator: Andrea Hoffmann
Client: Houston's Restaurant

Design Firm: Hoffmann & Angelic Design
Designer: Ivan Angelic
Calligrapher: Ivan Angelic
Client: Always An Adventure

Design Firm: Western Shores – Direct Marketing Group
Art Director: Brad Bennett (Bennett Design)
Calligrapher: Ivan Angelic
Illustrator: James Bowes
Client: B. C. Apples

Design Firm: Streamline Design Associates Inc.
Art Director: Andy Toxopeus
Designer: Andy Toxopeus
Calligrapher: Ivan Angelic
Client: Park Royal Shopping Center

Design Firm: Hoffmann & Angelic Design
Designers: Andrea Hoffmann & Ivan Angelic
Calligrapher: Ivan Angelic
Client: Calgary Tower

Design Firm: Streamline Design Associates Inc.
Art Director: Andy Toxopeus
Designer: Andy Toxopeus
Calligrapher: Ivan Angelic
Client: Crossroads Shopping Center

Design Firm: Hoffmann & Angelic Design
Calligrapher: Ivan Angelic
Client: Self-promotion

Design Firm: Hoffmann & Angelic Design
Art Director: Ivan Angelic
Designer: Andrea Hoffmann
Calligrapher: Ivan Angelic
Client: Hoffmann & Angelic Design

Design Firm: Hoffmann & Angelic Design
Designer: Andrea Hoffmann
Calligrapher: Ivan Angelic
Client: Hoffmann & Angelic Design

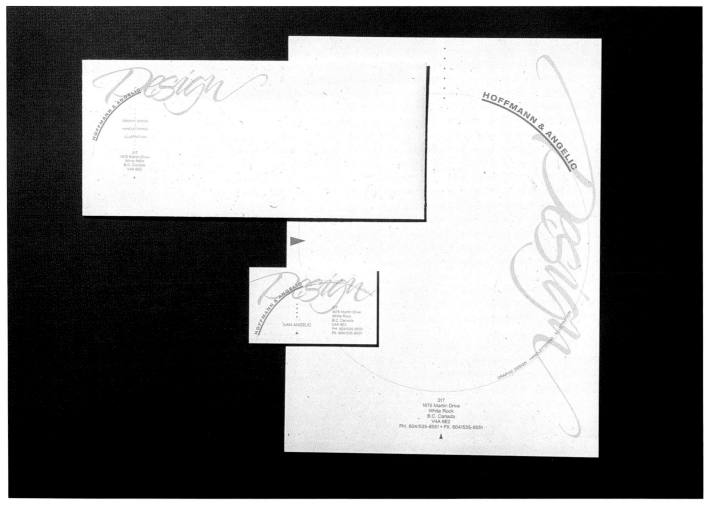

Design Firm: Hoffmann & Angelic Design
Art Director: Ivan Angelic
Designer: Andrea Hoffmann
Calligrapher: Ivan Angelic
Client: Hoffmann & Angelic Design

Design Firm: Hoffmann & Angelic Design
Art Director: Ivan Angelic
Designer: Andrea Hoffmann
Calligrapher: Ivan Angelic
Client: Business Partners

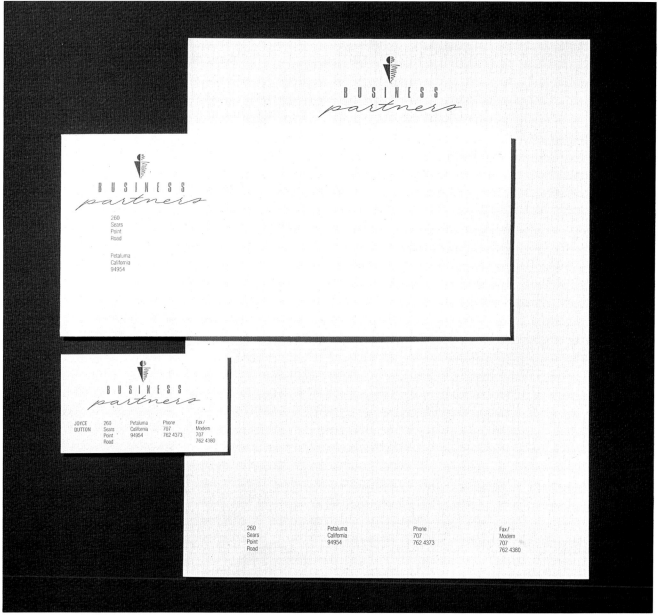

John Stevens

The work of John Stevens seems to take on a life of its own. It is as though he infuses it with a quality unique to itself that transcends the mere act of putting brush to paper. Even with the highly complex design for the *Reader's Digest* cover, the delicate script seems to speak subjectively of words and literature. This aspect of his work presents itself in the other pieces reproduced here (pages 95–99), showing again how real graphic communication reaches far beyond the technical skills of the artist.

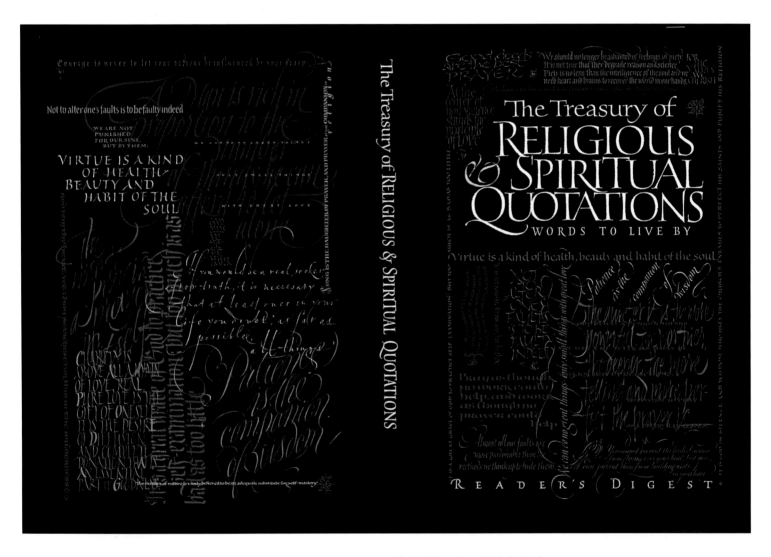

Art Director: Michele Perla
Designer: John Stevens
Calligrapher: John Stevens
Client: *Reader's Digest*

Art Director: Nanette Stevenson
Calligrapher: John Stevens
Illustration: Ed Young
Client: Northrop

Art Director: John Stevens
Calligrapher: John Stevens
Client: John Stevens

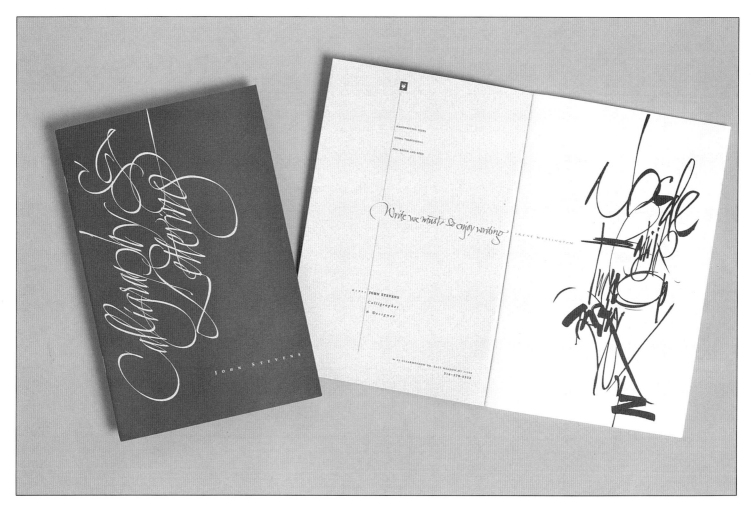

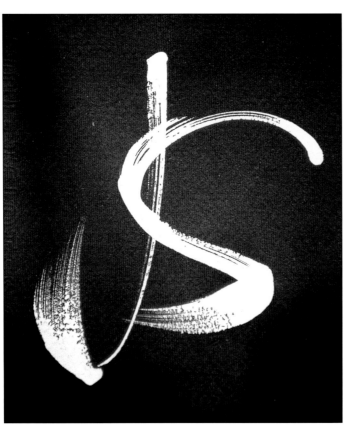

Calligrapher: John Stevens

Art Director: Joyce Teta
Calligrapher: John Stevens
Designer: John Stevens
Client: Calligraphy Centre

Art Director: Angela Skouras
Calligrapher: John Stevens
Photographer: Dan Borris
Client: *Rolling Stone*

Art Director: Vicki Kalajian
Calligrapher: John Stevens
Illustrator: Sandra Speidel
Client: Simon & Schuster

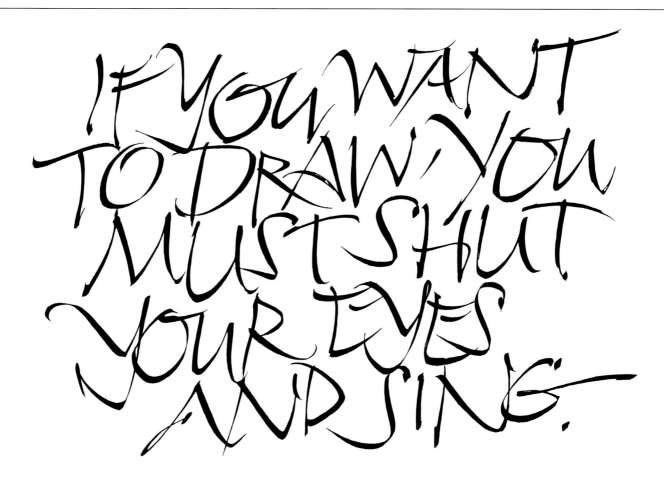

IF YOU WANT TO DRAW, YOU MUST SHUT YOUR EYES AND SING.

PABLO PICASSO

Calligrapher: John Stevens
Client: *Calligraphy & Lettering*

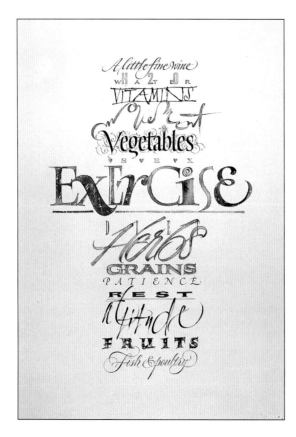

Design: John Stevens
Calligrapher: John Stevens
Client: Self-promotion

Design: John Stevens
Calligraphy: John Stevens
Illustration: John Stevens

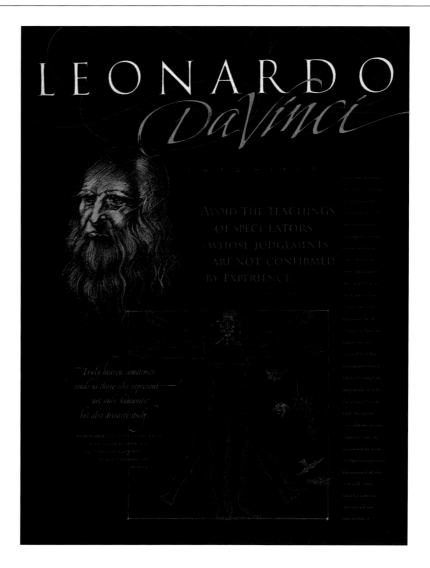

Design: John Stevens
Calligrapher: John Stevens
Client: Shared Medical Systems

Richard Lipton

Richard Lipton is an artist/calligrapher who also reaches for diversity of style within the demands of each given project. His catalog work (below) gives a sense of tradition and elegance, while his lettering for book covers (pages 101, 103) answers the expectations of publishers while retaining originality and character.

No 13

THE CARPET BAGS

THE ESSEX BAGS

(Top)
R49 Large Carpet Bag,
$295
(H 10" L 14" W 6½")
inside pocket with
credit card slots
hand-stitched handle
brass feet
detachable shoulder
strap with shoulder pad and
20" drop length

(Bottom left)
R48 Medium Carpet Bag,
$250
(H 9½" L 11 ¾" W 5 ¼")
inside pocket with
credit card slots
hand-stitched handle
brass feet

(Bottom center)
R47 Small Carpet Bag,
$190
(H 8" L 9" W 5")
inside pocket with
credit card slots
hand-stitched handle
brass feet

(Bottom right)
R46 Bicycle Bag,
$185
(H 7 ½" L 10" W 5")
inside pocket
adjustable gusset
adjustable shoulder strap
with 20" drop length

Art Director: Margorie Greene Millyard
Lettering Design: Richard Lipton
Photographer: Minh Nguyen
Client: Dooney and Bourke

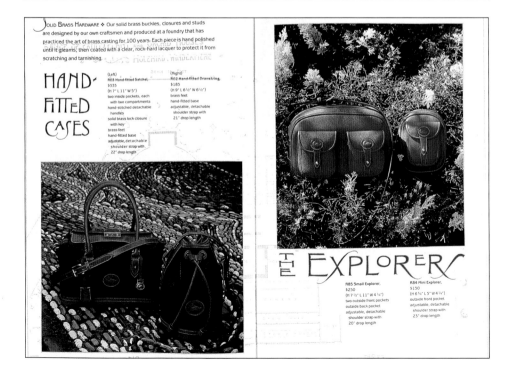

SOLID BRASS HARDWARE ❖ Our solid brass buckles, closures and studs are designed by our own craftsmen and produced at a foundry that has practiced the art of brass casting for 100 years. Each piece is hand polished until it gleams, then coated with a clear, rock-hard lacquer to protect it from scratching and tarnishing.

HAND-FITTED CASES

(Left)
R03 Hand-fitted Satchel,
$335
(H 7" L 11" W 5")
two inside pockets, each
with two compartments
hand-stitched detachable
handles
solid brass lock closure
with key
brass feet
hand-fitted base
adjustable, detachable
shoulder strap with
22" drop length

(Right)
R02 Hand-fitted Drawstring,
$185
(H 9" L 6 ½" W 6 ½")
brass feet
hand-fitted base
adjustable, detachable
shoulder strap with
21" drop length

THE EXPLORER

R85 Small Explorer,
$250
(H 7 ½" L 11" W 4 ¼")
two outside front pockets
outside back pocket
adjustable, detachable
shoulder strap with
20" drop length

R84 Mini Explorer,
$150
(H 6 ¾" L 5" W 4 ¼")
outside front pocket
adjustable, detachable
shoulder strap with
23" drop length

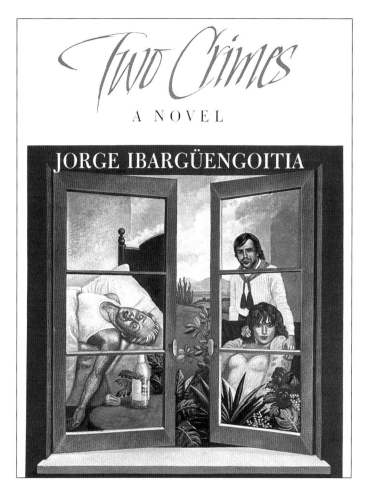

Art Director: William Lucky
Lettering Design: Richard Lipton
Client: David R. Godine

Art Director: William Lucky
Lettering Design: Richard Lipton
Illustrator: Dennis Corrigan
Client: David R. Godine

Art Director: Richard Lipton
Lettering Design: Richard Lipton
Client: Lipton Design

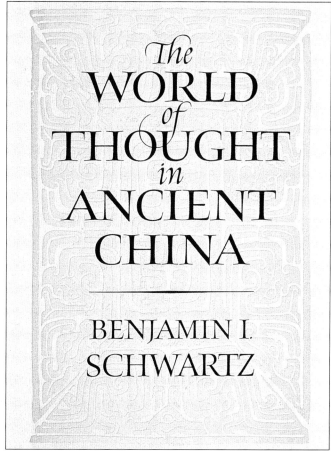

(top left)
Art Director: William Lucky
Lettering Design: Richard Lipton
Illustrator: Marci Gintis
Client: David R. Godine

(top right)
Art Director: Maryanne Perlak
Lettering Design: Richard Lipton
Client: Harvard University Press

Art Director: Christine Raquepaw
Lettering Design: Richard Lipton
Client: Beacon Press

James Fedor

Even though James Fedor uses many wonderful styles in his freehand work, he is one of the masters of the hand lettered script. Most of the pieces shown on pages 104–109 display some quality version of this. From book covers to magazine spreads there is great legibility and beauty in his work. These pieces show direct connection to the classical script form, and yet they do not look dated or out of place. Not an easy task to be sure.

Art Director: Dan Ishii, Dave Stratford
Designer: James H. Fedor
Client: Tahoe Telephone Directories/Kiwi Publishing

Design Firm: BYU Graphics
Art Director: Linda Sullivan
Lettering Design: James H. Fedor
Client: Utah Shakespearean Festival

Design Firm: Deseret Books
Art Director: Ralph Reynolds
Lettering Design: James H. Fedor
Client: Deseret Book Publishing Co.

Design Firm: Deseret Books
Art Director: Kent Ware
Lettering Design: James H. Fedor
Client: Deseret Book Publishing Co.

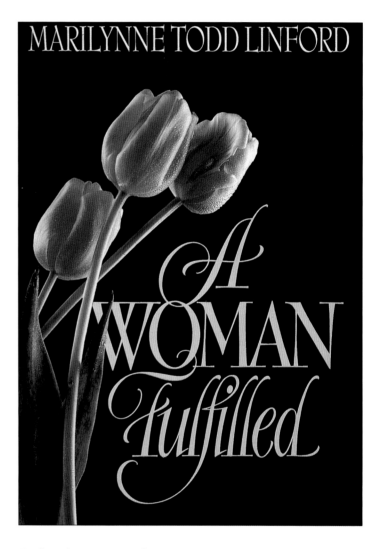

Design Firm: James Fedor Design, Inc.
Art Director: Jana Erickson (Bookcraft)
Designer: James H. Fedor
Client: Bookcraft, Inc.

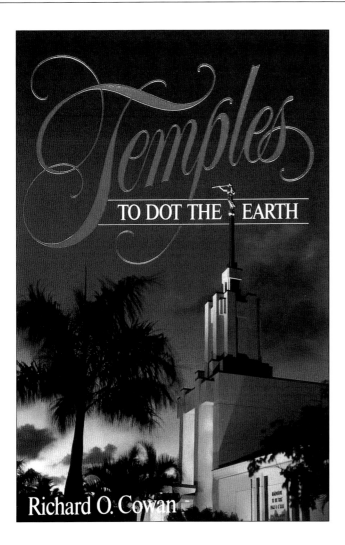

Design Firm: James Fedor Design, Inc.
Art Director: Jana Erickson (Bookcraft)
Designer: James H. Fedor
Client: Bookcraft, Inc.

Art Director: James H. Fedor
Designer: James H. Fedor
Client: Access Software, Inc.

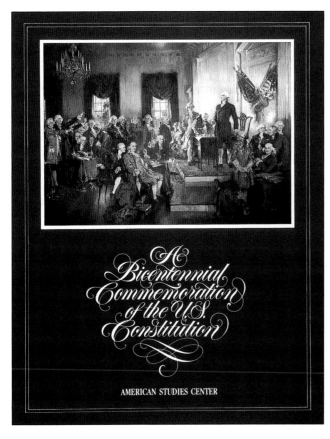

Design Firm: James Fedor Design, Inc.
Designer & Lettering Artist: James H. Fedor
Client: American Studies Center

Design Firm: New Era Design Studio
Art Director: Dileen Marsh
Lettering Artist: James H. Fedor
Client: New Era Magazine

Design Firm: New Era Design Studio
Art Director: Dileen Marsh
Lettering Artist: James H. Fedor
Client: New Era Magazine

Design Firm: New Era Design Studio
Art Director: Susan Lofgren
Lettering Artist: James H. Fedor
Client: New Era Magazine

Design Firm: Creative Source
Art Director: Doug Griffin
Lettering Design: James H. Fedor
Client: Weight Watchers

Georgia Deaver

Here is the application of hand script used to its ultimate effec-
tiveness. Georgia Deaver balances the width and heaviness of the
stroke with the art and the nature of each piece. This creates
careful studies that follow the intent and attitude of each idea. She
has created an interesting approach to her own stationery (below)
by redrawing the calligraphic part of her letterhead, business card,
etc., each time it is used. This obviously makes for extra work,
but the effect is always fresh and original.

Design Firm: Georgia Deaver Calligraphy Hand Lettering & Illustration
Art Director/Designer: Georgia Deaver
Client: Georgia Deaver Calligraphy Hand Lettering & Illustration

Design Firm: Britton Design
Art Director/Designer: Patti Britton
Illustration: Evans & Brown
Client: Viansa Winery

Design Firm: Fung Design
Art Director/Designer: Francis Fung
Client: San Francisco Grand Prix Association

Design Firm: Neugebauer Verlag
Art Director/Designer: Michael Neugebauer
Illustration: Chihiro Iwasaki
Client: Neugebauer Verlag

THE NEW WORLD RENAISSANCE BAND
Love Songs of the Renaissance

Design Firm: O'Neill Associates
Art Director/Designer: Kevin O'Neill
Illustration: *La Belle Dame Sans Merci,*
  by Sir Francis Dicksee 1853-1928
Client: Nightwatch Recording

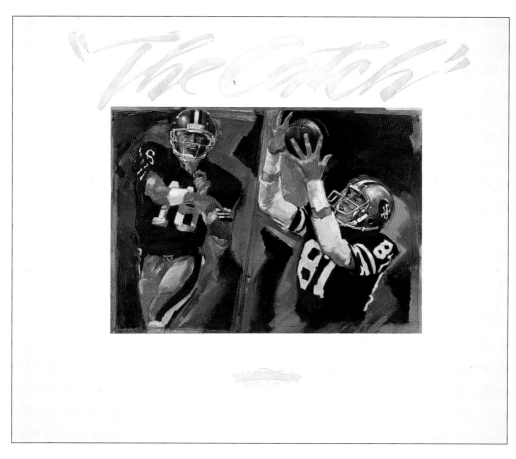

Design Firm: Authentic Impressions
Art Director/Designer: Frank Pollifrone
Illustrator: *Francis Livingston*
Client: Authentic Impressions

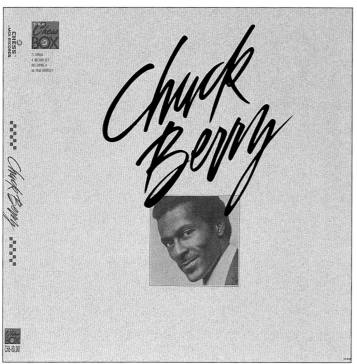

Design Firm: DZN, The Design Group
Art Director/Designer: Jim Emmerson
Client: MCA Records

Frank Riccio

Once again we see the illustrative freehand
stroke used as a significant graphic device. Frank
Riccio has a special touch in creating a textured
surface through his line and relating it to the
accompanying calligraphy. The series of initials
on page 115 create an unusual imagery, and the
"Worms and Other Parasites" art on this page
give a sense of old parchment through combining his art with textured background.

Art Director: James Walsh
Calligrapher: Frank Riccio
Illustrator: Frank Riccio
Client: *Emergency Medicine*

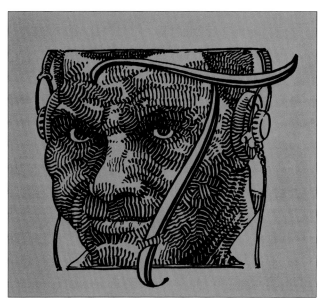

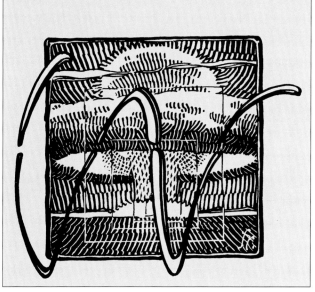

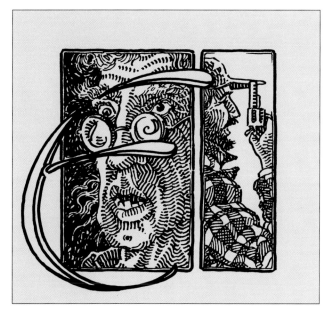

Calligrapher: Frank Riccio
Illustrator: Frank Riccio
Client: Kipling Press

(top)
Calligrapher: Frank Riccio
Illustrator: Frank Riccio
Client: Kipling Press

(bottom)
Calligrapher: Frank Riccio
Illustrator: Frank Riccio
Client: Helio Galleries

Calligrapher: Frank Riccio
Illustrator: Frank Riccio
Client: Self-promotion

Calligrapher: Frank Riccio
Illustrator: Frank Riccio
Client: Grace Publishing

Susan Skarsgard

The work of Susan Skarsgard is a wonderful combination of subtlety and movement. Much of this comes from her increased focus on her own personal fine art expression. As can be seen on pages 118–121, each of her examples could easily be integrated into a finished piece of fine art. Already an exquisite example of fine art is her treatment on page 119 of the letter "A" in her card series that she calls *Alphabet Fiction*.

Art Director: Dennis M. West
Calligrapher: Susan Skarsgard
Lettering Design: Susan Skarsgard
Client: *Calligraphy Review*

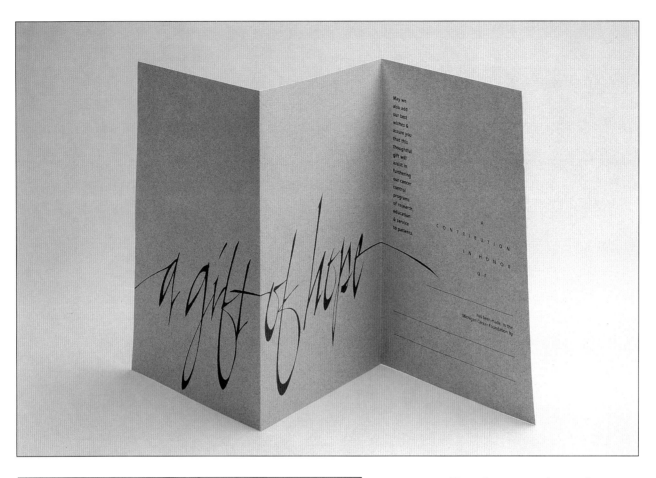

Calligrapher: Susan Skarsgard
Lettering Design: Susan Skarsgard
Client: Michigan Cancer Foundation

Calligrapher: Susan Skarsgard
Illustrator: Susan Skarsgard
Client: AIGA Book Show

Calligrapher: Susan Skarsgard
Client: Susan Skarsgard

Art Director: Wesley B. Tanner
Calligrapher: Susan Skarsgard
Client: The Book Club of California

Calligrapher: Susan Skarsgard
Client: Susan Skarsgard

Art Director: Nelson Greer
Calligrapher: Susan Skarsgard
Client: Mobil Masterpiece Theatre

Calligraphy: Susan Skarsgard
Client: Curley Campbell & Associates

Calligrapher: Susan Skarsgard
Client: Susan Skarsgard

Calligrapher: Susan Skarsgard
Client: Susan Skarsgard

Joey Hannaford

One of Joey Hannaford's talents is giving atmosphere to the imagery she's working with. Whether it is some accompanying piece of art or her own created letterforms, she injects a strategic attitude into the designs that clearly defines their content. "More Than Just a Story" has a wonderful mystical feeling to it, indicating that something other than just storytelling is involved here.

Art Director: Britt Taylor Collins
Lettering: Joey Hannaford
Client: Coral Key Publishing

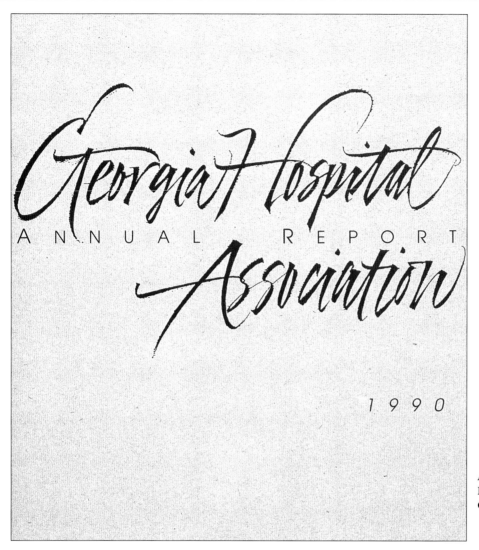

Art Director: Chuck Dalby
Lettering: Joey Hannaford
Client: Georgia Hospital Association

Art Director: Candy McGee
Lettering: Joey Hannaford
Art: (detail) "The Sunny South" by George Woltz
Courtesy of the Morris Museum, Agusta, GA
Client: Peachtree Publishers

Design Firm: Times 3
Art Director: Judith Martens
Lettering: Joey Hannaford
Client: Atlanta Symphony Orchestra

Art Director: Candy McGee
Lettering: Joey Hannaford
Client: Peachtree Publishers

Art Directors: Kevin Moore/Louise Britton
Lettering: Joey Hannaford
Client: Atlanta Symphony Orchestra

Agency: Larry Smith & Associates
Art Director: Larry Smith
Lettering: Joey Hannaford
Client: The Coca-Cola Company

Design Firm: Studio Graphica
Art Directors: Bob Clark/Joan Body
Lettering: Joey Hannaford
Illustrator: Walt Floyd
Client: Habitat for Humanity

Anthony Bloch

Here is the definitive urban touch of Anthony
Bloch. He has done many pieces for urban maga-
zines and cosmopolitan promotional spreads.
There is an accompanying strength and boldness to
his work even when the line is precise or delicate.
Readily recognizable, his work makes him very
accessible to the graphic design communities of
New York and other urban locations.

SPIKE LEE AND
MALCOLM X.

Art Director: Syndi Becker
Design Director: Robert Best
Photographer: Harry Benson
Client: *New York*

Art Director: Scott Yardley
Photographer: Margaret Gibbons
Client: *Red Book*

Art Director: Syndi Becker
Design Director: Robert Best
Photographer: Chris Callis
Client: *New York*

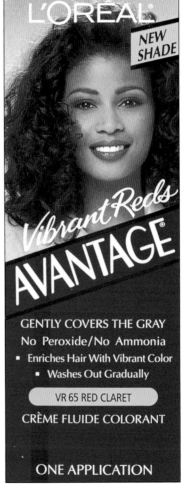

Design Firm: Lister Butler
Art Director: Alan Hill
Client: Molson

Art Director: Lauri Jean Phillips
Client: L'Oreal

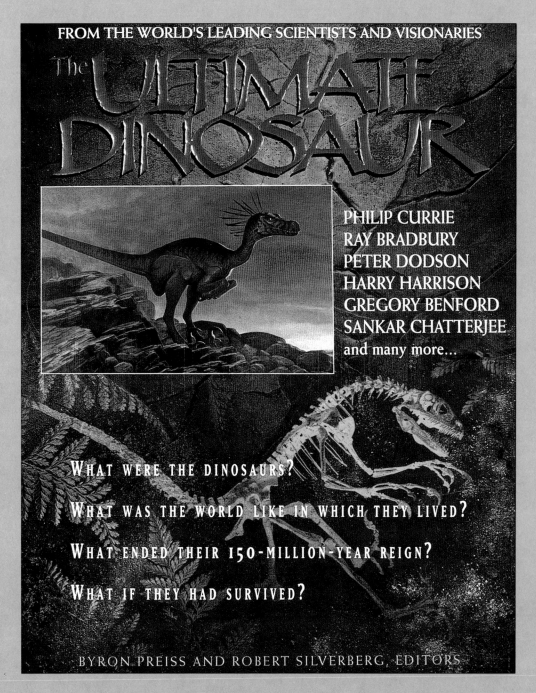

Design Firm: Byron Preiss Visual Publications
Art Director: Dean Motter
Photographer: Susan Goldman
Client: Bantam Books

Art Director: Janet Froelich
Photography: Mitch Epstein
Client: *New York Sunday Times Magazine*

Art Director: Syndi Becker
Design Director: Robert Best
Photographer: Peter Freed
Client: *New York*

Art Director/Designer: Anthony Bloch
Client: Self-promotion greeting card

Art Director: Amy Woodcox
Photographer: S. Peter Lopez
Client: *Palm Beach Life*

Nancy Culmone

Nancy Culmone's use of the freehand stroke in commercial application is directly related to her immersion in her own fine art expression. As can be seen in the logos and calligraphic lines reproduced on these pages (132–137), her deft hand easily articulates the messages, and her design sense in the placement of word and letterforms proves to be a strength as well. This can be readily seen in her "Wizard of Oz" T-shirt and her "Interaction" cover design.

Art Director: Judy Patterson
Calligrapher: Nancy Culmone
Photographer: David Bishop
Client: Bon Appetit Publishing

Art Director: Alwyn Velasquez
Calligrapher: Nancy Culmone
Client: D.C. Heath & Company

Calligrapher: Nancy Culmone
Client: Willow Hill School

Designer: Nancy Culmone
Calligrapher: Nancy Culmone
Client: Acton-Boxborough Community Education

Art Director: Susan Skarsgard
Designer/Calligrapher: Nancy Culmone
Client: Michigan Association of Calligraphers
Mohawk Paper Mills

Art Director: Grace Peters
Calligraphers: Nancy Culmone (Transformation)
Tom Costello (Tradition &)
Client: The Lettering Arts Guild of Boston

Design Firm:
Taplinger Publishing
Company
Art Director:
Paul Freeman
Calligrapher:
Nancy Culmone
Client:
The Society of Scribes,
New York

Designer: Nancy Culmone
Calligrapher: Nancy Culmone
Client: Self-promotion

Design Firm: Taplinger Publishing Company
Art Director: Edward Francolini
Calligrapher: Nancy Culmone
Client: The Society of Scribes, New York

Design Firm: Taplinger Publishing Company
Art Director: Valerie Bronsdon
Calligrapher: Nancy Culmone
Client: The Society of Scribes, New York

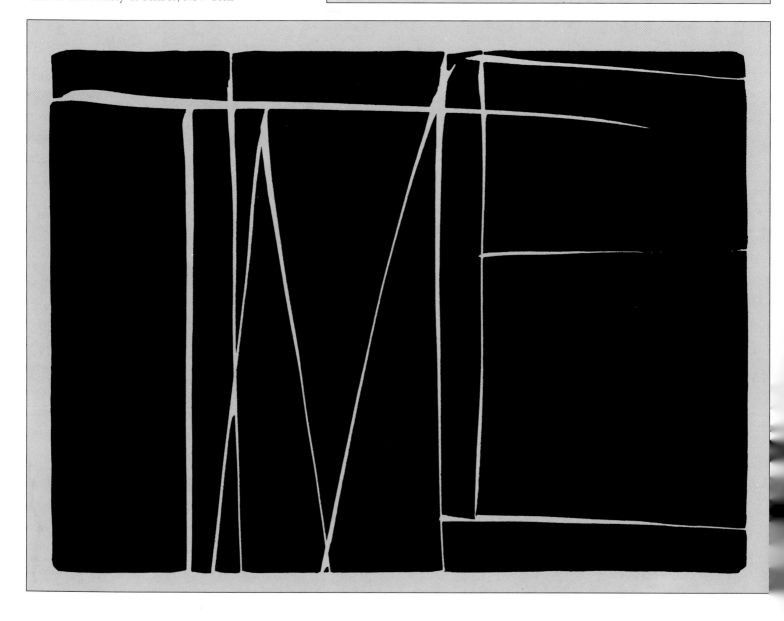

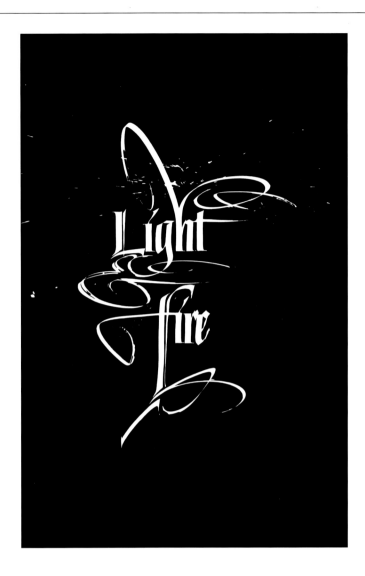

Designer: Nancy Culmone
Calligrapher: Nancy Culmone
Client: Self-promotion

Design Firm: Taplinger Publishing Company
Art Director: Edward Francolini
Calligrapher: Nancy Culmone
Client: The Society of Scribes, New York

Calligrapher: Nancy Culmone
Client: Eliza Tan & Ken DeMay

Raphael Boguslav

One of the unique aspects of the work of Raphael Boguslav is
the range of his expertise. His art reaches from the handsomely
rendered copperplate script (opposite) to the free whimsical
rough lettering (below) to the tightly drawn circle designs on
page 140. Each of these pieces represents a real feeling for
careful articulation and strong understanding of true letterforms.

Art Director: Marsha Cotner
Calligrapher: Raphael Bobuslav
Client: B. Altman's

Art Director: Kathey Wooley
Calligrapher: Raphael Boguslav
Client: Magratten Wooley

Art Director: Karen Smith
Calligrapher: Raphael Boguslav
Client: Turner Publishing

Art Director: Sabrina Brown
Calligrapher: Raphael Boguslav
Client: Brown Vandenbosch

Designer: Raphael Boguslav
Calligrapher: Raphael Boguslav
Client: Michael Gurian

Calligrapher: Raphael Boguslav
Client: John Mecray (John Mecray Editions)

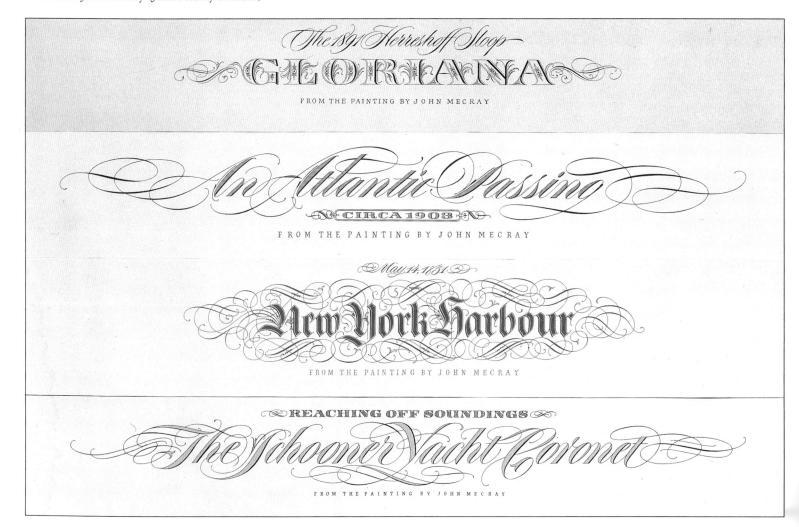

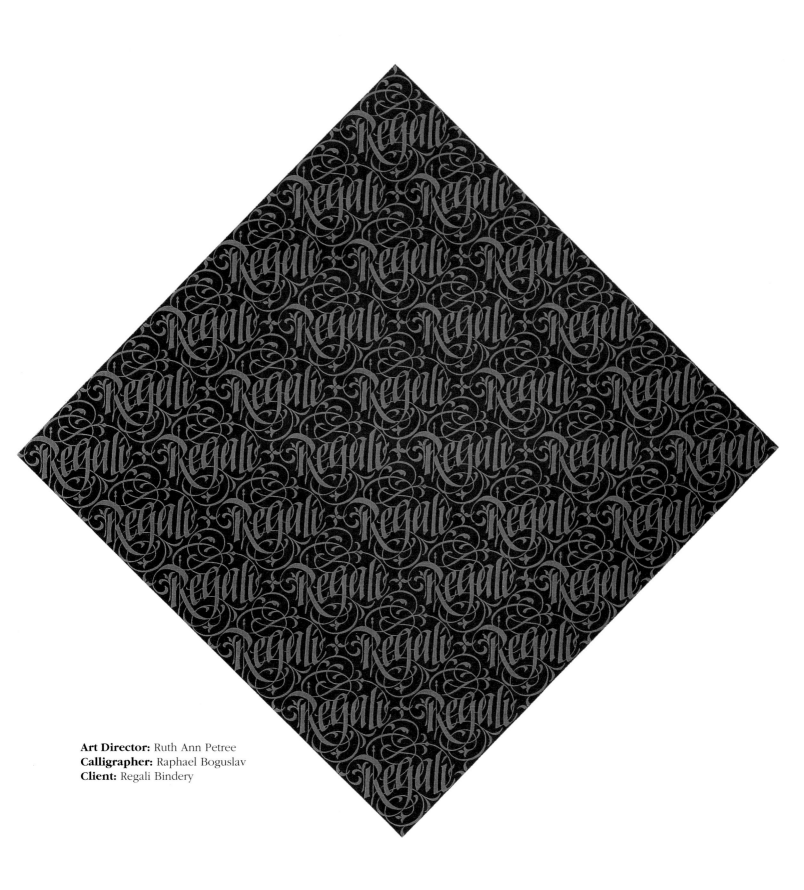

Art Director: Ruth Ann Petree
Calligrapher: Raphael Boguslav
Client: Regali Bindery

Bonnie Spiegel

Bonnie Spiegel is an accomplished calligrapher with many styles at her command. From the beautiful use of the Hebrew characters in the "Jonathan David" invitation cover to the bold self-promotion piece "The Studio" to the elegant script of "Symphonie Fantastique'" there is a sense of a broad reach of freehand styles. Thus she is able to accommodate many different design situations and give a specific style accent to a wide range of clients.

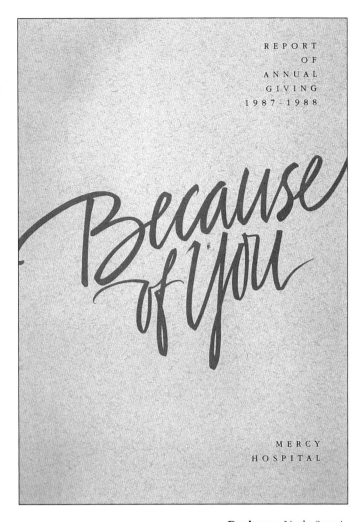

Designer: Linda Sturgis
Client: Mercy Hospital

Designer, Illustrator, Calligrapher: Bonnie Spiegel
Client: Portland Symphony Orchestra

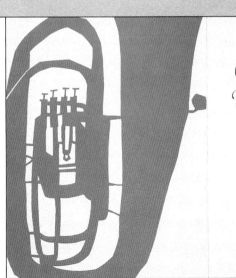

Designer/Calligrapher: Bonnie Spiegel
Client: Laura Horowitz

Designer/Calligrapher: Bonnie Spiegel
Client: Betty Novick

Designer/Calligrapher: Bonnie Spiegel
Client: Self-promotion

Designer: Camille Bush
Art: Map from the Osher Collection of USM by Henrichs Hondins
Client: The University of Southern Maine

Designer/Calligrapher: Bonnie Spiegel
Client: Self-promotion

Illustrators: Stephen Burr, Gary Symington
Client: Portland Chamber of Commerce Convention and Visitor's Bureau
      Barbara Whitten, Coordinator

Sheila Waters

Sheila Waters is a storyteller with her art. From her fanciful title for Willian Carlos Williams' *Portrait of a Lady* to the intricate designing of the Dylan Thomas work *Under Milkwood,* she has used her considerable talents to complement the telling of each story. This again is the use of subjective enhancement through art to more fully communicate the content of the stories. Her hand-drawn map and the invitation for the Library of Congress continue this marriage of art and text.

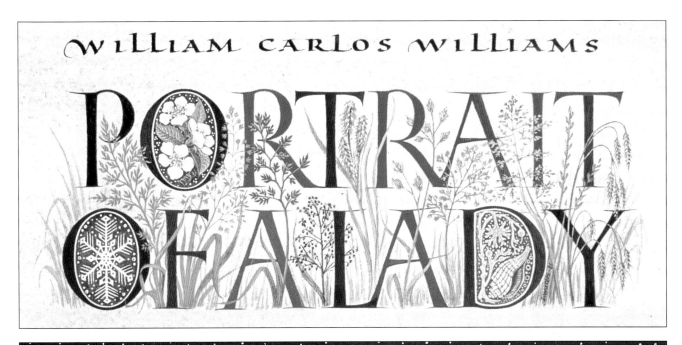

(top)
Calligrapher/Illustrator: Sheila Waters
Client: Glen & Karen Garlick

(bottom)
Calligrapher/Illustrator: Sheila Waters
Client: Sheila Waters

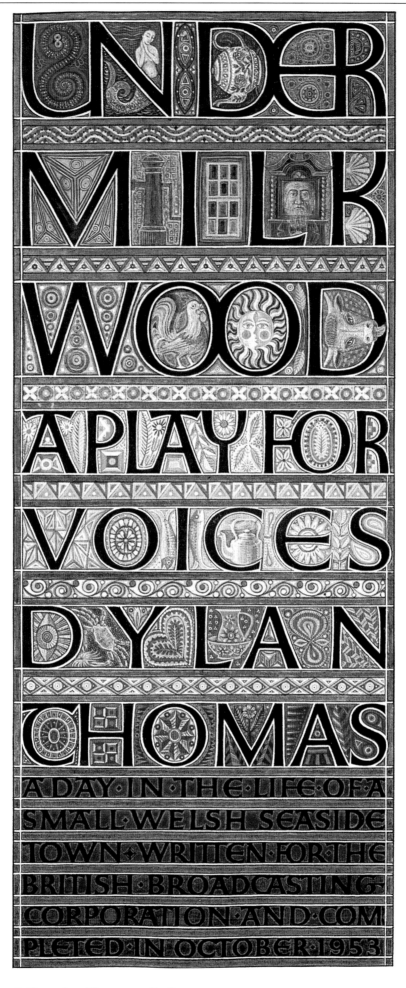

Calligrapher/Illustrator: Sheila Waters
Client: Edward Hornby

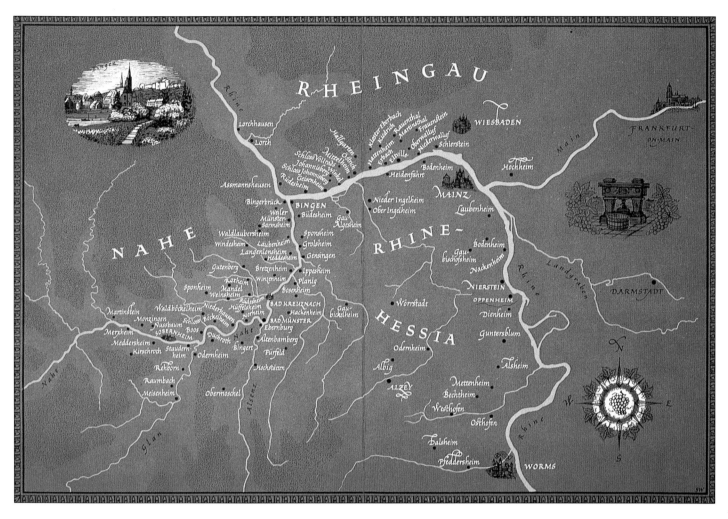

Art Director: Ruari McLean
Illustrator: Sheila Waters

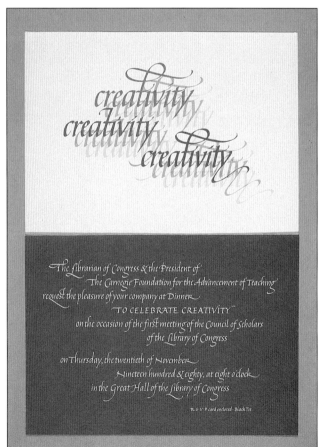

Art Director: John Michael
Calligrapher: Sheila Waters
Client: The Library of Congress

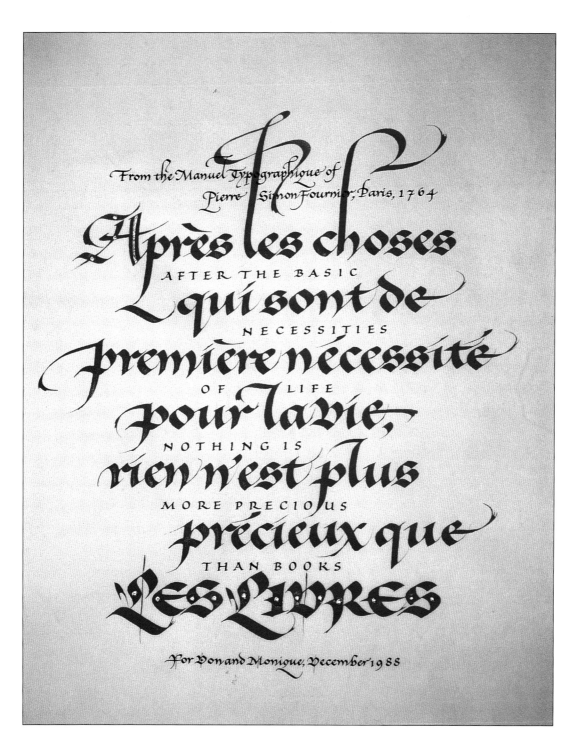

Calligrapher: Sheila Waters
Client: Donald & Monique Etherington

Calligrapher: Sheila Waters
Client: Sheila Waters

Brenda Walton

Brenda Walton's work has a wonderful sense of playfulness, whether it be the careful script on the *Pasta Gourmet* labels or the happy letterforms of her greeting cards. There is a genuine freshness and life to her styles and colors. Also, her development of the words "Celebration" and "Thanksgiving" fits well with their general connotation.

Design Firm: Peggy Koch
Designer: Peggy Koch
Client: SBG Partners

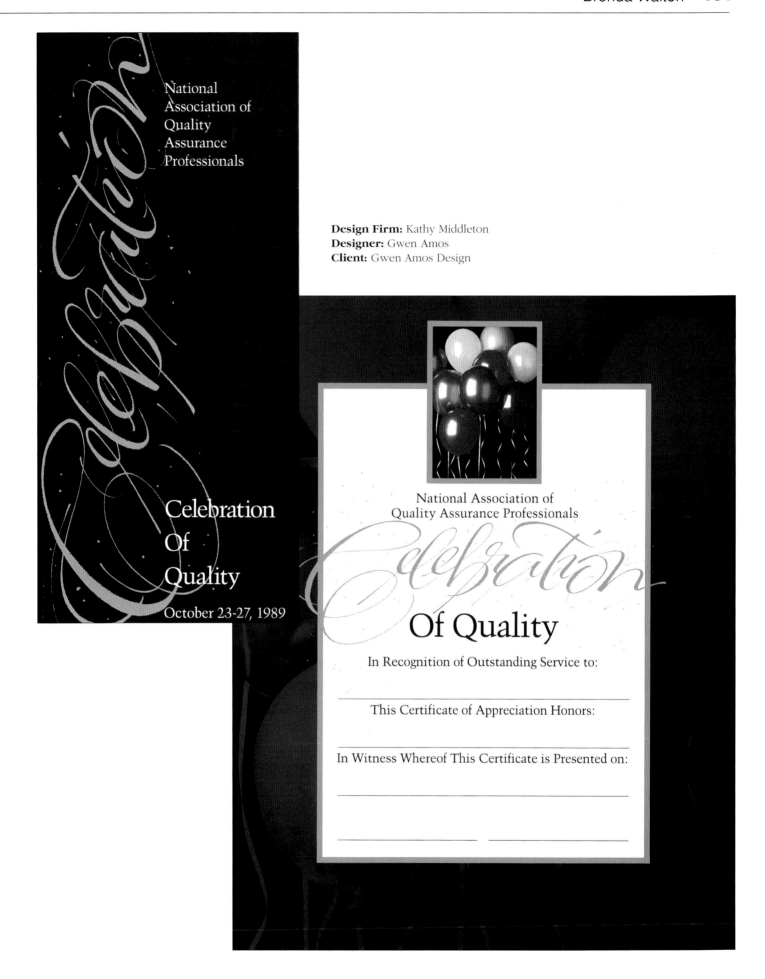

National
Association of
Quality
Assurance
Professionals

Design Firm: Kathy Middleton
Designer: Gwen Amos
Client: Gwen Amos Design

Celebration
Of
Quality

October 23-27, 1989

National Association of
Quality Assurance Professionals

Of Quality

In Recognition of Outstanding Service to:

This Certificate of Appreciation Honors:

In Witness Whereof This Certificate is Presented on:

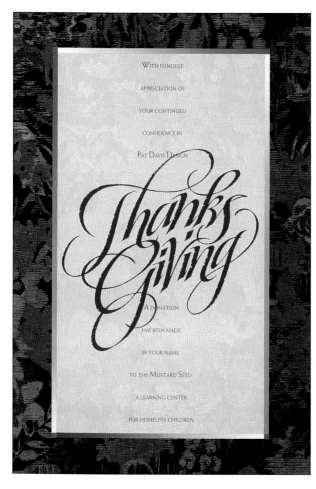

Design Firm: Kathy Middleton
Designer: Pat Davis
Client: Pat Davis Design

Design Firm: Paula Sugarman
Designer: Paul Page
Client: Page Design

Design Firm: Brenda Walton
Designer: Sandra McMillan
Client: Marcel Schurman Company

Design Firm: Brenda Walton
Designer: Sandra McMillan
Client: Marcel Schurman Company

Design Firm: Brenda Walton
Designer: Susan Birnbaum
Client: Marcel Schurman Company

Iskra Johnson

Iskra Johnson's work is evocative and eye-catching and finds its way into many different projects. Many book covers, posters, and other promotional pieces have her distinctive imprint on them. As can be seen in the work on these next five pages, her style is varied and ranges from tight rendering to free-stroke lettering.

Art Director/Designer: Braldt Bralds
Calligrapher: Iskra Johnson
Illustrator: Braldt Bralds
Client: United Nations Environmental Programme

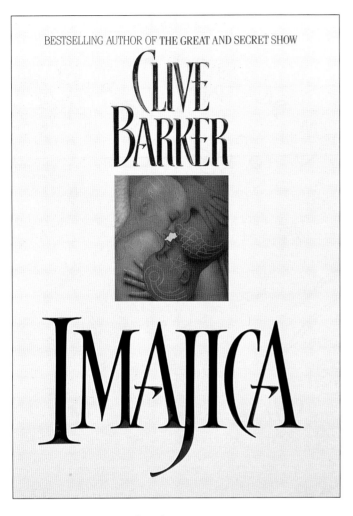

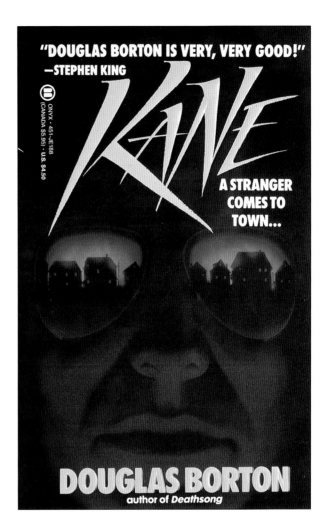

Art Director: Gene Mydlowski
Calligrapher: Iskra Johnson
Illustrator: Kirk Reinert
Client: Harper Collins Publishers

Art Director: George Carnell
Calligrapher: Iskra Johnson
Client: New American Library

Art Director: Jo DiDonato
Calligrapher: Iskra Johnson
Photographer: Reisig & Taylor
Client: Sony Music

Art Director/Designer: Dirk Mynatt
Calligrapher: Iskra Johnson
Client: Ralph Golan, M.D.

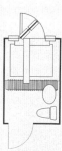

There's an austere beauty to the Laurel Canyon section of Los Angeles that, to some who live there, brings to mind the rustic charm of rural Japan. In response to that setting, designer/builder and original owner Russ Leland remodeled a dark, 6-by-12-foot bathroom to capture the feeling of bathing outdoors in nature—a Japanese ideal.

In place of a small window, Leland "opened out the wall" with a shoji-like aluminum-framed door and windows. Terrazzo covers interior walls and a low partition bisecting the room to form the bathing area.

"It's minimalist," says actor John Castellanos, who shares the house with television producer Rhonda Friedman, "but it gives you just what you need"—qualities of which a Zen master would no doubt approve.

Opposite: A remodeled Los Angeles bath gets a view of the home's tranquil setting through a window wall. For privacy without loss of view, a fiberglass-mesh screen may be lowered. Marble planks form a tray across the terrazzo tub. **Above:** A simple niche holds toiletries. Green porcelain echoes the landscape just outside.

ZEN
AND
THE
ART
OF THE
BATH

120 April 1992

Art Director: Ragnar Johnsen
Calligrapher: Iskra Johnson
Photographer: Tim Street-Porter
Client: *Home*

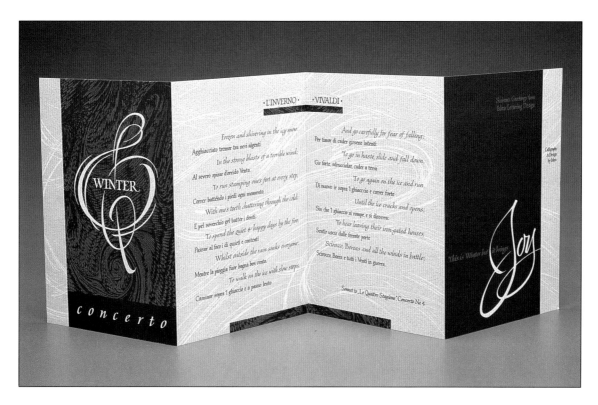

Art Director/Designer: Iskra Johnson
Client: Iskra Johnson

Design Firm: Belyea Design
Art Director: Patricia Belyea
Calligrapher: Iskra Johnson
Photographer: Rosanne Olson
Client: Impression Northwest

Design Firm: The Davis Group
Art Director: Chris Barbee
Calligraphy: Iskra Johnson
Client: Nintendo

Design Firm: Burrier Lorenzo
Art Director: Burrier Lorenzo
Calligrapher: Iskra Johnson
Client: The Broadway Market

Design Firm: Iskra Johnson
Client: Portfolio

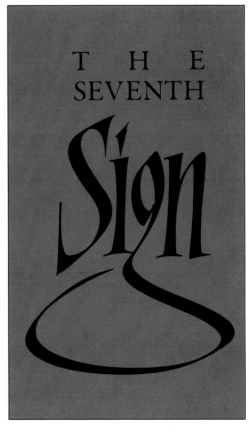

Design Firm: Seiniger Advertising
Art Director: Olga Kaljakin
Calligraphy: Iskra Johnson
Client: Movie Studio

Miscellany

The following is a compilation of additional pieces created by other artists from around the world. This work is of the same high quality, and it would surely be a dereliction of duty not to include it. It represents the creative output of many inspired artists who hold to the same creative concerns that were previously discussed in this book. The author was impressed with the submissions received for this project, and found it extremely difficult to select the work to be included. In fact, some pieces of real merit were excluded only for lack of space. This is an uncomfortable but glorious position to be in: see here the results of that difficult process of selection.

Design Firm: Puccinelli Design
Art Director: Keith Puccinelli
Designer: Heidi Palladino
Illustrator: Heidi Palladino
Client: California Avocado Festival

Design Firm: Puccinelli Design
Art Director: Keith Puccinelli
Designer: Heidi Palladino
Illustrator: Heidi Palladino
Client: Pucinelli Design:
Original Reproductions

Design Firm: Modern Dog
Art Director: Cheryl Zahniser,
Michael Strassburger
Designer: Michael Strassburger
Illustrator: Michael Strassburger
Client: Nordstrom

Design Firm: Leland Design
Art Director: Allan Zukor
Illustrator: Lori Leland
Client: Allan Zukor Advertising Design

Design Firm: Rominar Graphic Design
Art Director: Robert W. Minarik
Designer: Robert W. Minarik
Illustrator: Robert W. Minarik
Client: Keith Samuels

Design Firm: Rominar Graphic Design
Art Director: Robert W. Minarik
Designer: Robert W. Minarik
Illustrator: Robert W. Minarik
Client: Maison Blanche

Design Firm: Salvo Design
Art Director: Ken Salvo
Designer: Ken Salvo
Illustrator: Ken Salvo
Client: Kona Kai Farms

Design Firm: Muller & Company
Art Director: John Muller
Designer: Mike Miller
Client: Kansas City Jazz Commission

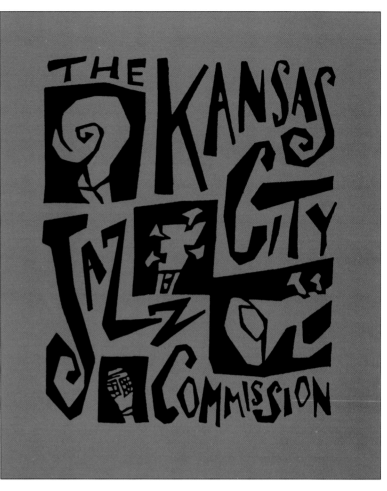

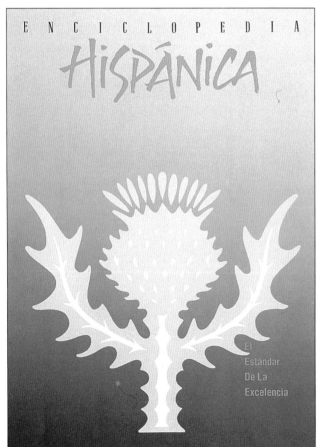

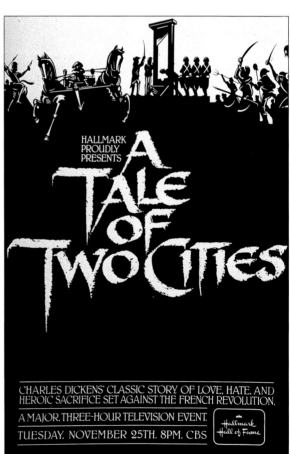

Design Firm: Hill & Knowlton.
Art Director: Mary Ackerby
Lettering Artist: Holly Dickens
Client: Encyclopedia Hispanica

Design Firm: Tribune TV Guide
Lettering Artist: Holly Dickens
Client: Hallmark/Tribune

Design Firm: Ema Design
Art Director: Thomas C. Ema
Designer: Debra Johnson Humphrey
Illustrator: Thomas C. Ema
Client: Artist's Angle

Design Firm: Muller & Company
Art Director: John Muller
Designer: Jane Weeks
Client: Milano

Design Firm: Tharp Did It
Art Director: Rick Tharp, Cerstin Chatham
Letterer: Rick Tharp
Illustrator: Susan Jaekel
Client: Body Chemistry by Diane Richardson

Design Firm: Tharp Did It
Designer/Illustrator: Rick Tharp
Client: Sebastiani Vineyards

Design Firm: Ema Design
Art Director: Thomas C. Ema
Designer: Debra Johnson Humphrey
Illustrator: Thomas C. Ema
Client: Artist's Angle

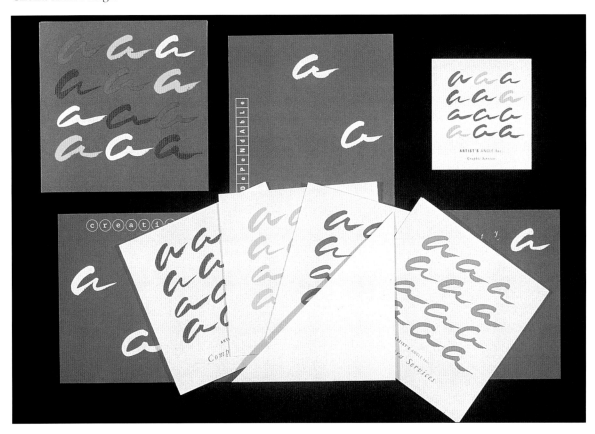

Design Firm: Mark Oliver Design, Inc.
Illustrator: Holly Dickens
Client: Nexxus Hair Products

Design Firm: Sharon Musikar
Graphic Design
Art Director: Sharon Musikar
Designer: Sharon Musikar
Client: Self-promotion

ESTATE
BOTTLED

Clos La Chance

SANTA CRUZ MOUNTAIN

1 9 9 0 **CHARDONNAY**

Design Firm: Tharp Did It
Designer: Rick Tharp
Illustrator/Calligrapher: Jana Heer
Client: Clos LaChance Vineyard

Design Firm: Segura Inc.
Art Director: Carlos Segura
Designer: Carlos Segura
Client: Illusion/Jim Beam

Design Firm: Tharp Did It
Designer: Rick Tharp
Illustrator: Georgia Deaver
Client: Sebastiani Vinyards

Design Firm: Tharp Did It
Art Director: Rick Tharp
Designer: Patricia Belyea
Calligrapher: Georgia Deaver
Client: Sabastiani Vinyards

Design Firm: Packaging Design
Art Director: G. Italo Marchi
Client: "IL MANGIA" Industria Dolciaria
(Siena) Italia

Design Firm: Jim Lange Design
Designer: Jim Lange
Client: Jim Lange

Design Firm: Richard Emery Design, Inc.
Art Director: Richard Emery
Designer: Richard Emery
Client: Logo for Project Adventure, Inc.

Design Firm: Animus Comunicacao
Art Director: Rique Nitzsche
Designer & Stroke: Rique Nitzsche
Illustrator: Duiu (Landscapes of the Letterhead)
Client: Renasce

Design Firm: Animus Comunicacao
Art Director: Rique Nitzsche
Designer: Rique Nitzsche
Illustrator: Rique Nitzsche
Client: Animus Comunicacao

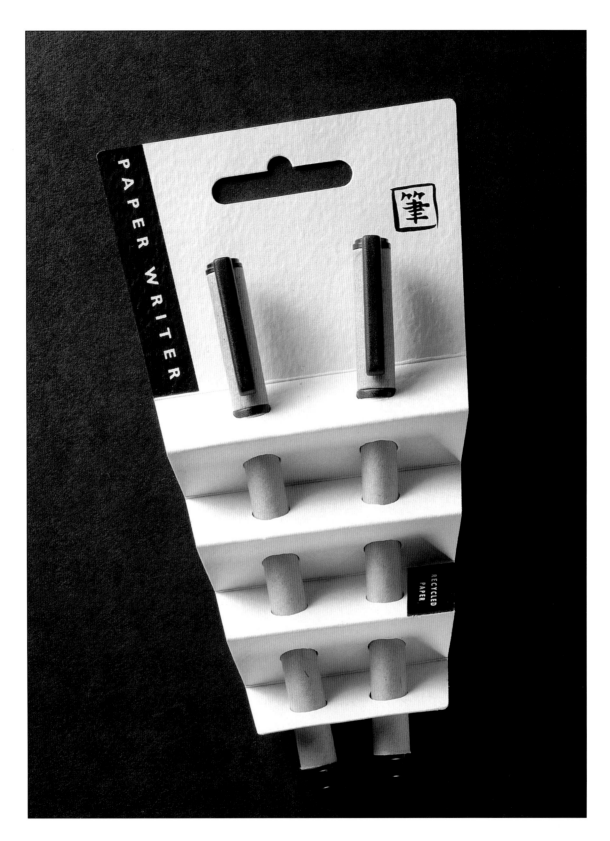

Design Firm: P. I. Design Consultants
Art Director: Don Williams
Designer: Don Williams
Illustrator: Tracey Wilkinson
Client: Danny Pollock Products

The

Second

Sound

Of

The

Shofar

New Year's Card
Designer: Stan Brod
Client: Stan Brod

Design Firm: Lipson Alport Glass & Associates
Art Director: Herb Lubalin
Designer: Stan Brod
Illustrator: Stan Brod
Client: *U & lc.*

Design Firm: Barrett Design Inc.
Art Director: Karen Dendy
Designer: Karen Dendy
Client: Exos Inc.

Design Firm: Group Four Design
Designer: John Philion
Lettering Artist: Holly Dickens
Client: Jhirmack Hair Products

Design Firm: Cannon S.A.
Art Director: Jorge Daniel Soler
Designer: Jorge Daniel Soler
Client: Lander

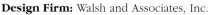

Design Firm: Walsh and Associates, Inc.
Art Director: Miriam Lisco
Designer: Miriam Lisco, Katie Dolejsi, Michael Stearns
Calligrapher: Glenn Yoshiyama
Client: Misty Ridge Winery

Design Firm: Walsh and Associates, Inc.
Art Director: Miriam Lisco
Designer: Katie Dolejsi
Calligrapher: Glen Yoshiyama
Client: Sweet Mouthful Speciality Foods

Designer: Annie Cicale
Client: Folk Art Center, Southern
Highlands Handicraft Guild

Designer: Annie Cicale
Client: Folk Art Center, Southern
Highlands Handicraft Guild

Gallery

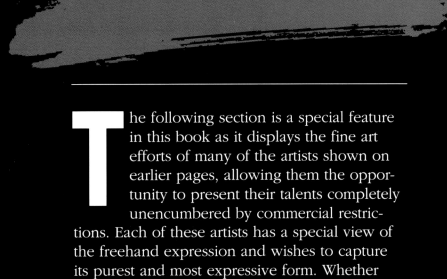

The following section is a special feature in this book as it displays the fine art efforts of many of the artists shown on earlier pages, allowing them the opportunity to present their talents completely unencumbered by commercial restrictions. Each of these artists has a special view of the freehand expression and wishes to capture its purest and most expressive form. Whether creating their art just for themselves of for a commission from a second party, they have the freedom to use the free brushstroke and penstroke in a completely unrestricted way. This allows the experience of pure self expression. As was stated in *The Creative Stroke 1*, This section also allows the viewer an opportunity to discover ideas and applications that could be equally viable in commercial situations even though they were conceived as personal expression in fine art. This section is an important and necessary conclusion for a book on the beauty and scope of freehand expression in graphics.

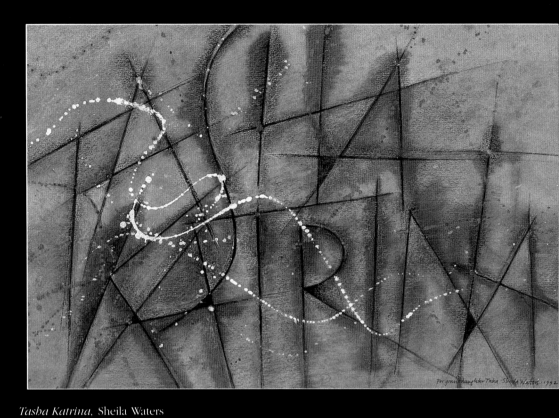

Tasha Katrina, Sheila Waters

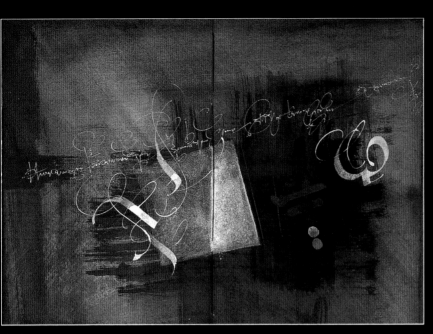

Red Routes, Suzanne Moore,
From the collection of the
Mortimer Rare Book Room,
Smith College

Alphabet Watercolor, Brenda Walton

No Snowflake Falls, Joey Hannaford

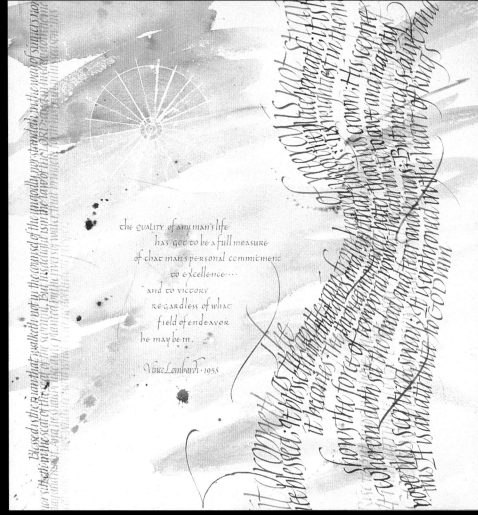

the QUALITY of any man's life
    has got to be a full measure
    of that man's personal commitment
        to excellence…
    and to victory
        regardless of what
        field of endeavor
        he may be in.

        Vince Lombardi · 1958

Quality, Joey Hannaford

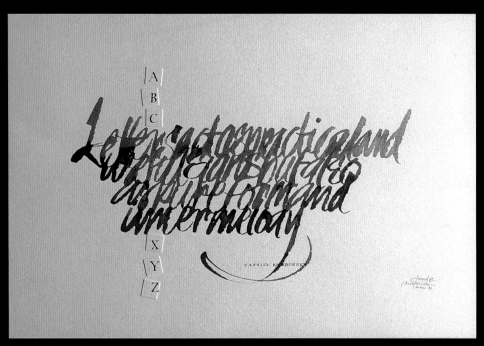

*"Letters act as practical and useful signs but also as pure form and
inner melody" (Vassily Kandinsky)*, Claude Dieterich A.

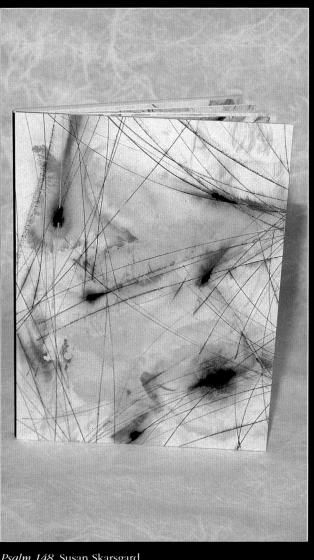

Psalm 148, Susan Skarsgard

'K' from *Alphabetic Fiction: 26 Paintings*, Susan Skarsgard

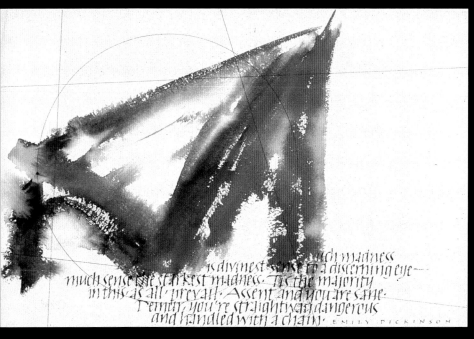

Much Madness (1980), Jean Evans

Star Light Night: The Letter Arts Network, Marsha Brady

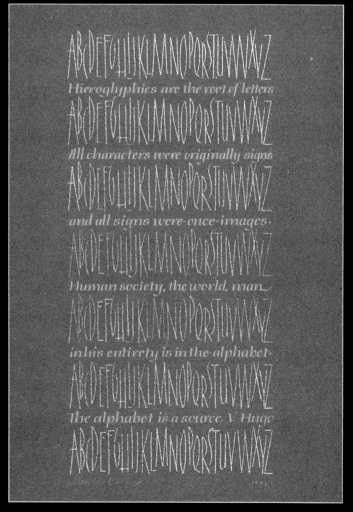

The Alphabet is a Source: Collection of Erena Rae, Marsha Brady

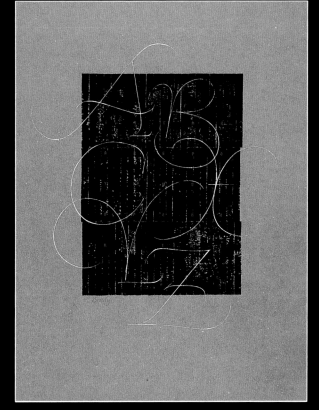

Sator, Larry Brady

WE SHALL NOT CEASE FROM EXPLORATION
AND THE END OF ALL OUR EXPLORING
WILL BE TO ARRIVE WHERE WE STARTED
AND KNOW THE PLACE FOR THE FIRST TIME.
THROUGH THE UNKNOWN REMEMBERED GATE
WHEN THE LAST OF EARTH LEFT TO DISCOVER
IS THAT WHICH WAS THE BEGINNING;
AT THE SOURCE OF THE LONGEST RIVER
THE VOICE OF THE HIDDEN WATERFALL
AND THE CHILDREN IN THE APPLE-TREE
NOT KNOWN BECAUSE NOT LOOKED FOR
BUT HEARD, HALF-HEARD, IN THE STILLNESS
BETWEEN TWO WAVES OF THE SEA.
QUICK NOW, HERE, NOW, ALWAYS—
A CONDITION OF COMPLETE SIMPLICITY
(COSTING NOT LESS THAN EVERYTHING)
AND ALL SHALL BE WELL AND
ALL MANNER OF THING SHALL BE WELL
WHEN THE TONGUES OF FLAME ARE INFOLDED
INTO THE CROWNED KNOT OF FIRE
AND THE FIRE AND THE ROSE ARE ONE.

T.S. Eliot, Larry Brady

"Beauty" Leon Battista Alberti (1452), Howard Glasser

To Hammer Out, Stan Brod

Running Deer, Stan Brod

THREE TRIANGLES
OF BIRDS
CROSSED THE ENORMOUS OCEAN
STRETCHED OUT IN WINTER LIKE A SINGLE GREEN BEAST

EVERYTHING LIES FLAT THE SILENCE THE
EXTENDED GREY
THE HEAVY LIGHT OF DAY THE
INTERMITTENT EARTH

OVER THE FLIGHT OF DARK
EVERYTHING AND BIRDS
ANOTHER FLIGHT
WINTERY BODIES TREMBLING TRIANGLES WHOSE
WINGS JUST BARELY MOVING CARRY FROM ONE
PLACE TO THE NEXT ON THE COASTS
OF CHILE THE GREY CHILL THE DESOLATE
DAYS

I AM HERE
WHILE
FROM SKY TO SKY
THE
SHIVER OF
MIGRATING
BIRDS
LEAVES ME
SUNK IN MYSELF
AND IN
MY FLESH
AS IN A
PERPETUITY OF
DUG BY A
MOTIONLESS
SPIRAL

I FACE THE EMPTINESS I AM

IT IS THE BODY OF
WINTER STRETCHED OUT
AND THE SEA HAS
SLIPPED OVER
ITS BLUE FACE
A BITTER MASK.

Three Triangles: Pablo Neruda, Jane Dill

Two things Fighting, Maybe Three, Gretchen Marical

Index

Ivan Angelic
Hoffmann & Angelic Design
317-1675 Martin Dr.
White Rock, B.C. V4A6E2
Canada

Patricia Belyea
Belyea Design
1809 7th Ave. Ste 1007
Seattle, WA 98101

Anthony Bloch Calligraphy
Design
854 W. 181 St.
New York, NY 10033

Raphael Boguslav
50 Old Beach Rd. A2
Newport, RI 02840

Larry and Marsha Brady
Brady Design
11561 Harrisburg Rd.
Los Alamitos, CA 90720

Sherry Bringham
1804 Arlington Ave.
El Cerrito, CA 94530

Stan Brod
2401 Ingleside Ave.
Cincinnati, OH 45206

Annie Cicale
68 Sigmon Rd.
Fletcher, NC 28732

Colleen
25 Stanton Rd.
Brookline, MA 02146-6806

Nancy Culmone
P.O. Box 1425
Littleton, MA 01460-4425

Georgia Deaver
1045 Sansome St., Suite 311
San Francisco, CA 94111

Karen Dendy
Barrett Design
545 Concord Ave.
Cambridge, MA 02138

Holly Dickens
612 N. Michigan Ave.
Chicago, IL 60611

Claude Dieterich A.
1417 Cabrillo St.
San Francisco, CA 94118

Jane Dill
123 Townsend St., 606
San Francisco, CA 94107

Thomas C.Ema
Ema Design
1228 Fifteenth St., 301
Denver, CO 80202

Richard S. Emery
Richard Emery Design, Inc.
79 Eastern Ave.
Essex, MA 01929

Jean Evans
142 Garden St.
Cambridge, MA 02138

James Fedor
1645 South Artistic Circle
Bountiful, UT 84010

Howard Glasser
28 Forge Rd.
Assonet, MA 02707

Joey Hannaford
Hannaford Designs
675 Drewry St. Studio 4
Atlantic, GA 30306

Iskra Johnson
Iskra Lettering Design
1605 12th #26
Seattle, WA 98122

Jim Lange Design
203 N. Wabash Ave.
Chicago, IL 60601

Lori Leland
Leland Design
1151 Carver Place
Mountain View, CA 94040

Richard Lipton
26 Mather St.
Dorchester, MA 02124

Terry Louie
3550 19th St.
San Francisco, CA 94110

G. Italo Marchi
Via L. Rizzo - 81
Perugia, Italy

Gretchen Maricak
1040 Chapin
Birmingham, MI 48009

Mike Miller
Muller & Company
4739 Belleview
Kansas City, MO 64112

Robert W. Minarik
RoMinar Graphic Design
900 Laurie Lane
St. Gabriel, LA 70776

Suzanne Moore
P.O. Box 477
Ashfield, MA 01330

Sharon Musikar
7524 Indian Hills Dr.
Rockville, MD 20855

Rique Nitzsche
Animus Comunicao
Ladeira Do Ascurra 115A
22241-320/Rio/RJ
Brazil

Heidi Palladino
Puccinelli Design
114 E. De La Guerra #5
Santa Barbara, CA 93101

Mike Quon
Mike Quon Design Office
568 Broadway #703
New York, NY 10012

Daniel Riley
Riley Design Associates
214 Main St. Suite A
San Mateo, CA 94401

Frank Riccio
33 Eames Boulevard
Black Rock, CT 06605

Ken Salvo
Salvo Design
1204 Boulevard Way
Walnut Creek, CA 94595

John Sayles
Sayles Graphic Design
308 Eighth St.
Des Moines, IO 50309

Carlos Segura
Segura Inc.
361 W. Chestnut
Chicago, IL 60010

Paul Shaw
Paul Shaw Letter Design
785 West End Ave.
New York, NY 10025

Susan Skarsgard
807 Hutchins St.
Ann Arbor, MI 48103

Jorge Daniel Soler
Cannon S.A.
Salguero 550
(M77) Buenos Aires
Argentina

Bonnie Spiegel
121 William St.
Portland, ME 04103

John Stevens
53 Clearmeadow Dr.
E. Meadow, NY 11554

Michael Strassburger
Modern Dog
601 Valley St. No. 309
Seattle, WA 98109

Rick Tharp
Tharp Did It
50 University Ave. #21
Los Gatos, CA 94030

Edward Vartanian
Edward Vartanian Design
114 Capuano Ave.
Cranston, RI 02920

Brenda Walton
Calligraphy & Illustration
14 Midway Ct.
Sacramento, CA 95817

Julian Waters
23707 Woodfield Rd.
Gaithersburg, MD 20882

Sheila Waters
20740 Warfield Ct.
Gaithersburg, MD 20879

Jane Weeks
Muller & Company
4739 Belleview
Kansas City, MO 64112

Tracey Wilkinson
P.I. Design Consultants
1-5, Colville Mews
Lonsdale Rd.
London W112AR

Glenn Yoshiyama
Walsh and Associates, Inc.
4464 Fremont Ave. N. #310
Seattle, WA 98103